University
of Michigan
Business
School Management Series

INNOVATIVE SOLUTIONS TO THE
PRESSING PROBLEMS OF BUSINESS

The mission of the University of Michigan Business School Management Series is to provide accessible, practical, and cutting-edge solutions to the most critical challenges facing businesspeople today. The UMBS Management Series provides concepts and tools for people who seek to make a significant difference in their organizations. Drawing on the research and experience of faculty at the University of Michigan Business School, the books are written to stretch thinking while providing practical, focused, and innovative solutions to the pressing problems of business.

Also available in the UMBS series:

Becoming a Better Value Creator, by Anjan V. Thakor

Achieving Success Through Social Capital, by Wayne Baker

Improving Customer Satisfaction, Loyalty, and Profit,
by Michael D. Johnson and Anders Gustafsson

The Compensation Solution, by John E. Tropman

Strategic Interviewing, by Richaurd Camp, Mary Vielhaber,
and Jack L. Simonetti

Creating the Multicultural Organization, by Taylor Cox

Getting Results, by Clinton O. Longenecker and
Jack L. Simonetti

A Company of Leaders, by Gretchen M. Spreitzer and
Robert E. Quinn

For additional information on any of these titles or future titles
in the series, visit www.umbsbooks.com.

Executive Summary

Assuring high performance in an increasingly complex world requires good management of unexpected threats that can escalate out of control. Traditional managerial practices such as planning are designed to protect organizations from potentially disruptive events. But they often make things worse. There are other sources of remedy, but they come from an unexpected sector—from a group of "exotic" organizations called high reliability organizations (HROs).

HROs such as nuclear power plants, aircraft carriers, and wildland firefighting crews warrant closer attention from managers and organizational leaders because they operate under trying conditions yet experience fewer than their fair share of problems. These organizations have developed ways of acting and styles of leading that enable them to manage the unexpected better than most other kinds of organizations. The ways in which they do this are a template for all organizations that want to be more reliable.

HROs manage the unexpected through five processes: (1) preoccupation with failures rather than successes, (2) reluctance to simplify interpretations, (3) sensitivity to operations, (4) commitment to resilience, and (5) deference to expertise, as exhibited by encouragement of a fluid decision-making system. Together these five processes produce a collective state of *mindfulness*. To be mindful is to have a rich awareness of discriminatory detail and an enhanced ability to discover and correct errors that could escalate into a crisis. These five processes are the fundamentals that are the basis of improvements in quality, reliability, and productivity in any organization.

This book enables managers and organizational leaders to focus on developing and strengthening the HRO processes that are weakest in their organization. Chapter One previews the case for mindfulness through an in-depth look at how the Union Pacific Railroad mismanaged the unexpected under trying conditions and suggests how organizations such as aircraft carriers and nuclear power plants would have handled things differently. The common thread, missing from the UP case, is sustained, candid mindfulness that updates one's grasp of what is happening. Chapter Two illustrates the rudiments of the unexpected and mindfulness by using flight operations on aircraft carriers as the anchor. The chapter underscores the importance of doubt, inquiry, and updating. Chapter Three uses nuclear power generation as the anchor to describe in detail how the five HRO processes work together to produce mindfulness and how traditional management practices undermine mindfulness.

The remaining chapters enable readers to put this analysis into action in their own organizations. Chapter Four draws the strands of the argument together and provides an audit for analyzing the state and quality of mindfulness in any organization. Chapter Five shows how to move an organizational culture toward more mindful management of the unexpected. Finally, Chapter Six shows how managers can make their own style of managing more mindful.

Managing the Unexpected

Assuring High Performance in an Age of Complexity

Karl E. Weick
Kathleen M. Sutcliffe

JOSSEY-BASS
A Wiley Company
www.josseybass.com

Published by

 JOSSEY-BASS
A Wiley Company
989 Market Street
San Francisco, CA 94103-1741

www.josseybass.com

Jossey-Bass books and products are available through most bookstores. To contact Jossey-Bass directly, call (888) 378-2537, fax to (800) 605-2665, or visit our website at www.josseybass.com.

Substantial discounts on bulk quantities of Jossey-Bass books are available to cor-porations, professional associations, and other organizations. For details and dis-count information, contact the special sales department at Jossey-Bass.

We at Jossey-Bass strive to use the most environmentally sensitive paper stocks avail-able to us. Our publications are printed on acid-free recycled stock whenever possible, and our paper always meets or exceeds minimum GPO and EPA requirements.

Library of Congress Cataloging-in-Publication Data

Weick, Karl E.
Managing the unexpected: assuring high performance in an age
  of complexity / Karl E. Weick, Kathleen M. Sutcliffe.—1st ed.
  p. cm.—(University of Michigan Business School
management series)
Includes bibliographical references and index.
  ISBN 0-7879-5627-9 (alk. paper)
  1. Crisis management. 2. Leadership. 3. Industrial
management. I. Sutcliffe, Kathleen M., date- II. Title. III.
Series.
  HD49 .W45 2001
  658.4'056—dc21

2001001341

FIRST EDITION
HB Printing   10 9 8 7 6 5 4 3

Contents

Series Foreword

Welcome to the University of Michigan Business School Management Series. The books in this series address the most urgent problems facing business today. The series is part of a larger initiative at the University of Michigan Business School (UMBS) that ties together a range of efforts to create and share knowledge through conferences, survey research, interactive and distance training, print publications, and new media

It is just this type of broad-based initiative that sparked my love affair with UMBS in 1984. From the day I arrived I was enamored with the quality of the research, the quality of the MBA program, and the quality of the Executive Education Center. Here was a business school committed to new lines of research, new ways of teaching, and the practical application of ideas. It was a place where innovative thinking could result in tangible outcomes.

The UMBS Management Series is one very important outcome, and it has an interesting history. It turns out that every year five thousand participants in our executive program fill out a marketing survey in which they write statements indicating the most important problems they face. One day Lucy Chin, one of our administrators, handed me a document containing all these statements. A content analysis of the data resulted in a list of forty-five pressing problems. The topics ranged from growing a company to managing personal stress. The list covered a wide territory, and I started to see its potential. People in organizations tend to be driven by a very traditional set of problems, but the solutions evolve. I went to my friends at Jossey-Bass to discuss a publishing project. The discussion eventually grew into the University of Michigan Business School Management Series— Innovative Solutions to the Pressing Problems of Business.

The books are independent of each other, but collectively they create a comprehensive set of management tools that cut across all the functional areas of business—from strategy to human resources to finance, accounting, and operations. They draw on the interdisciplinary research of the Michigan faculty. Yet each book is written so a serious manager can read it quickly and act immediately. I think you will find that they are books that will make a significant difference to you and your organization.

Robert E. Quinn, Consulting Editor
M.E. Tracy Distinguished Professor
University of Michigan Business School

Preface

When Bob Quinn first talked to us about the University of Michigan Business School's Pressing Problems initiative and showed us a list of what executives thought were their forty-five most pressing problems, we nodded, "That's interesting," and went on about our business. At the time "our business" was a reexamination of the data concerning how people organize for high performance in settings where the potential for error and disaster is overwhelming. We were looking at nuclear aircraft carriers, air traffic control systems, aircraft operations, hostage negotiation, emergency medical treatment, nuclear power generation, continuous processing firms, and wildland firefighting crews. These diverse organizations share a singular demand: They have no choice but to function reliably. If reliability is compromised, severe harm results. Adopting the controversial terminology first used at Berkeley, we lumped these organizations together and called them *high reliability organizations* (HROs).

Other people who had examined these organizations were struck by their unique structural features. We saw something else: These organizations also think and act differently. But whereas their processes were different, they were not uniquely different.

And that's where Bob's Pressing Problems list comes back into play. What impressed us was that those forty-five problems, almost without fail, involved a lapse in reliability. Either somebody counted on something to happen and it didn't, or someone counted on something not to happen and it did. And most of those pressing problems—problems such as failures to think and plan strategically, or to maintain a high-performance climate—did not emerge full-blown. Instead, clues had been accumulating for some time that small, unexpected things were happening and weren't going away. Problems were building up. *Passing* problems were thus turning into *pressing* problems.

■ Benchmarking Against the Experts

Why didn't more people see this? And why wasn't managing the unexpected at the top of executives' list of pressing problems? One obvious reason is that managers don't talk in abstractions the way professors do. *Managing the unexpected* is the language of the general, not the concrete. So fault the professors for that one. But fault the managers for the next reason: Managers love to benchmark, but they love to benchmark the familiar. Get them too far from their comfort zone with a stretch organization or a stretch metaphor, and they are quick to retreat behind the judgment, "That's irrelevant!" If you think about it, that's not exactly what people have in mind when they talk about a *learning organization*. Bold initiatives come from bold generalizing. Bold generalizing is clearly evident in the recent enthusiasm among surgeons, fire fighters, and product development champions to embrace *crew resource management* (CRM). CRM was developed in the airline industry and is about better communication among flight crews. Surgeons aren't pilots, nor are crew chiefs or product champions. Nevertheless, they do all succeed or fail depending on their relationships. And they look to the experts to learn how to improve their relating. They benchmark on the experts in a process, not on the experts in a look-alike firm.

We invite you to benchmark on the experts in reliability. This book is about experts in assured high performance and how they stay on top of operations, despite repeated interruptions. Part of their success in managing the unexpected stems from their uncommon success in finding ways to stay *mindful* about what is happening. They update their ideas of what is happening and are not trapped by old categories or crude renderings of the contexts they face. They use techniques that you can copy—techniques that are worth copying because they ensure faster learning, more alert sensing, and better relationships with customers. Unreliable suppliers and unreliable services make us crazy. But much to our surprise, reliability does not mean a complete lack of variation. It's just the opposite. It takes *mindful variety* to assure stable high performance. HROs have learned that the hard way. We hope to make it easier for you to learn the same lessons they learned the hard way.

■ Acknowledgments

Several people figured in this project and we want to acknowledge with appreciation their help. This work is informed by a host of valued colleagues whose work we admire, people such as Charles Perrow, John Carroll, Gene Rochlin, Eli Berniker, Lee Clarke, Scott Sagan, Paul Schulman, Todd LaPorte, Andrew Hopkins, James Reason, Gary Klein, Diane Vaughan, Paul Goodman, Alfie Marcus, Mary Nichols, Tom Mercer, Bob Bea, and especially "the mother of HROs" Karlene Roberts. David Gaba, Steve Small, Don Berwick, David Van Straelen, Bob Wears, and Marilynn Rosenthal have helped us understand adverse events in medical settings. K.E.W. has learned a great deal about managing the unexpected from members of the wildland firefighting community, including Ted Putnam, Dave Thomas, Paul Gleason, Paul Linse, Jason Greenlee, Jim Cooke, and Mark Linane. K.M.S. has learned to accept the unexpected with humor and grace from people who have no choice but to show up and manage it all, including Shannon Anderson, Anjali Sastry, Carolen Hope, Gail Marnik, and Frances Sanders. David Obstfeld played an important role in helping us synthesize early ideas. JoAnn Sokkar gave us both invaluable bibliographic help in tracking down sources. John Bergez taught us about the virtues of writing directly to our readers, and we are grateful for what he taught us.

Finally, two people cleared space and time so we could immerse ourselves in this project. Karen Weick is a seasoned and beloved expert at managing the unexpected, and half of this book is directly traceable to her efforts. The other half of the book is traceable to the totally unexpected Tim Wintermute, who for K.M.S. makes it all worthwhile. We dedicate this book to both of them with love!

May 2001   Karl E. Weick
Ann Arbor, Michigan   Kathleen M. Sutcliffe

Managing the Unexpected

Managing the Unexpected

What Business Can Learn from High Reliability Organizations

One of the greatest challenges any business organization faces is dealing with the unexpected. For example, a leading manufacturer of integrated circuits expects to boost competitiveness by dramatically improving quality and doubling capacity, but it unexpectedly finds its share price falling as customers switch to the new products being offered by its competitors. A premier forest products firm continues production during a normal trough in the business cycle, only to be surprised by a deeper and more long-lasting trough than they ever expected. The responsible manager of the largest corporate division of a consumer products firm suddenly realizes that his market has been conquered by a certain competitor—a development that his subordinates suspected had been building steadily for several years. As these examples show, the unexpected doesn't take the form of a major crisis. Instead, it is triggered by a deceptively simple sequence in organizational life: A person or unit has an intention, takes action, misunderstands the world; actual events fail to coincide with the intended sequence; and there is an unexpected outcome.[1] People dislike unexpected outcomes and surprises. Because of that, they sometimes make situations worse. That's the tragedy that motivates this book.

We suspect that the inability to manage the unexpected lies behind a number of the pressing problems that executives face. Problems, after all, occur either when something that we expected to happen fails to happen or something that we did not expect to happen does happen. For example, consider the chief concerns of today's business professionals reported in the first annual (2000) University of Michigan Business School Pressing Problems survey. The second most frequent problem executives reported was "thinking and planning strategically"; the third most pressing problem was "maintaining a high-performance climate." From our perspective, both these problems are variants of one that is the focus of this book, *dealing with unexpected events*. Whether the issue is strategy or performance, problems become more pressing when expected strategy and performance outcomes fail to materialize or when unexpected impediments to strategy and performance materialize. Either scenario is a brush with the unexpected. And in either case people often take too long to recognize that their expectations are being violated and that a problem is growing more severe. Moreover, once they belatedly recognize that the unexpected is unfolding, their efforts at containment are misplaced.

In general, people can manage unexpected events poorly, in which case the events spiral, get worse, and disrupt ongoing activity; or they can manage them well, in which case the events shrink and ongoing activity continues. How you can improve your organization's management of the unexpected is the subject of this book.

What does it mean to manage an unexpected event well? Good management of the unexpected is *mindful* management of the unexpected. That answer comes from careful study of organizations that operate under very trying conditions all the time and yet manage to have fewer than their fair share of accidents. These organizations, which are referred to collectively as *high reliability organizations* (HROs), include power grid dispatching centers, air traffic control systems, nuclear aircraft carriers, nuclear power generating plants, hospital emergency departments, and hostage negotiation teams. The better of these organizations rarely fail even though they encounter numerous unexpected events. They face an "excess" of unexpected events because their technologies are complex and their constituencies are varied in their demands—and because the people who run these systems, like all of us, have an incomplete understanding of their own systems and what they face.

We attribute the success of HROs in managing the unexpected to their determined efforts to act *mindfully*. By this we mean that they organize themselves in such a way that they are better able to notice the unexpected in the making and halt its development. If they have difficulty halting the development of the unexpected, they focus on containing it. And if some of the unexpected breaks through the containment, they focus on resilience and swift restoration of system functioning.

When we call this approach *mindful*, we mean that HROs strive to maintain an underlying style of mental functioning that is distinguished by continuous updating and deepening of increasingly plausible interpretations of what the context is, what problems define it, and what remedies it contains. The key difference between HROs and other organizations in managing the unexpected often occurs in the earliest stages, when the unexpected may give off only weak signals of trouble. The overwhelming tendency is to respond to weak signals with a weak response. Mindfulness preserves the capability to see the significant meaning of weak signals and to give strong responses to weak signals. This counterintuitive act holds the key to managing the unexpected.

This book is grounded in the assumption that high reliability organizations enact on a larger scale what all of us try to do well on a much smaller one. We can all get better at managing the unexpected if we pay more attention to those who have no choice but to do it well. In this first chapter we will illustrate this argument by taking a close look at how the Union Pacific Railroad mismanaged the unexpected during its merger with the Southern Pacific Railroad and ended up gridlocking significant portions of its transportation system. We argue that Union Pacific got into trouble because it failed to use any of the five processes that enable HROs to manage the unexpected mindfully. The five processes are previewed briefly in this chapter; linked with expectations, blind spots, and mindfulness in Chapter Two; described in fuller detail in Chapter Three; formatted as an organizational audit for use by executives and managers in Chapter Four; interpreted as the infrastructure of a safety culture in Chapter Five; and translated into a set of practical guidelines for action in Chapter Six.

■ Union Pacific Mismanages the Unexpected

"An old brakeman faces his ultimate test." This breathless headline in the October 6, 1997, issue of *Business Week*[2] signaled the failure of Union Pacific CEO Richard Davidson to manage the unexpected when Union Pacific (UP) merged with Southern Pacific (SP). The Surface Transportation Board had unanimously approved the merger in August 1996 because it promised to bring the vaunted expertise of UP to bear on the badly deteriorating SP. Not long after the formal acquisition on September 11, 1996, the vaunted "expertise" of the UP began to unravel. Unexpected events came in waves. And the responses only made things worse.

Mismanaging the People

The expectation that safe operation would continue on the merged system proved to be unfounded. In the first eight months of 1997, four employees were killed in railyard accidents. Between June 22 and September 11, 1997, the railroad experienced six major collisions that killed another five employees and two trespassers.[3] Sixty federal regulators started riding the trains and watching dispatchers as a result of these accidents.[4] Among other findings, they found that crews were on duty longer than allowed by law, equipment had not been maintained, and dispatchers were unfamiliar with regions to which they had been assigned. These conditions were due in large part to swift cuts in personnel shortly after the merger. As a result of these cuts, fatigue, poor maintenance, and slow dispatching had become issues because management underestimated the number of people needed to run the merged railroad. For example, on October 29, in Navasota, Texas, a southbound freight from North Platte, Nebraska, moving at twenty-five miles per hour, smashed into the rear of a stopped unit rock train. There were no serious injuries, but evidence suggested that the engineer and conductor on the North Platte train had gone on duty after only eight hours of rest and had fallen asleep.[5]

Equally surprising was the dramatic shift of sentiment on the part of shippers, particularly in the Gulf Coast area. Those who had endorsed the merger now found themselves confronted by delays that got worse and worse, shipments that were lost altogether and couldn't be traced, and expensive truck transportation as their only remaining option. Shippers were badly hurt when the average speed of trains dropped from nineteen to twelve miles per hour. This is a severe drop because it equates to a loss of 1800 locomotives, or about one-fourth of the UP fleet.[6] The dramatic loss of speed was often a moot point since growing numbers of trains didn't move at all. They were stuck in sidings without locomotives, which had been removed to solve power shortages elsewhere.[7] For example, at one point the Bailey Yard in North Platte, Nebraska, found itself 161 locomotives short of the number needed to power the trains that were expected to leave that yard in just the next twenty-four hours. Trains that did have locomotives still couldn't move because they were manned by crews whose duty time had expired while they waited for clearance to move the train. "On the morning of October 8, systemwide, 550 freights stood still for lack of engines or crews."[8] Since all the sidings were full with backed up trains, movement on the single track mainline was possible in only one direction. There was no place where a train going in one direction could pull over into a siding and allow a train moving in the opposite direction to pass. Since most of the trains on the mainline were pointed toward Houston, they could not move aside to allow movements in the opposite direction away from Houston. The system was gridlocked as far away as Chicago.

Mismanaging the Operations

Much of this meltdown could be traced to one spot, the Englewood classification yard in Houston.[9] When SP ran this facility, they kept it moving at its capacity of 3,500 cars by workarounds that involved moving some of the classification to satellite yards at Strang and Beaumont, and by sorting some cars down line, away from yards, by a technique called block-swapping. This tactic involved sending trains with cars for mixed destinations "in the same direction in close order. Down the line they swapped blocks of cars to form solid trains for three destinations—for East St. Louis, Memphis, and Pine Bluff."[10] When UP took over the operation of Englewood, they moved all this satellite classification back to the Englewood yard, where it could be centralized and "done in the right way."[11] Trains began backing up the very next day. On October 27, Englewood locked up with 6,179 cars in the yard.[12] UP sent more managers and more engines to break the logjam, but all this did was plug up the system even more.

What makes all this so puzzling is that it occurred on the watch of a self-proclaimed "operations guy." Davidson had been a railroader all his life. He had been vice president of operations for Union Pacific in 1982 when the UP merged with the Missouri Pacific Railroad. Davidson had been courted by the Burlington Northern in 1994 to straighten out its operations problems. And yet here is Davidson, finally the top person at the railroad, and he can't get the trains to run on time. Why not?

You begin to get a clue if you examine the list of reasons given by top management to explain why service had become so rotten. The postmerger problems were variously attributed to blizzards in the Midwest, customs backups at the Mexican border, unexpected track work, flash floods, derailments, a surge in plastics traffic, Hurricane Danny, poorly maintained SP equipment, and inherited labor agreements. In the eyes of top management, UP and its system were the victims, not the culprits. Not a good sign.

But not a rare sign either.[13] Executives often manage the unexpected by blaming it on someone, usually on someone else. This happens with sufficient frequency that it qualifies as a pressing problem in its own right. But there are other issues in managing the unexpected that are visible in the Union Pacific example.

Mismanaging the Strategy

The Union Pacific clearly had a growth strategy in place. Just two years before formalizing the SP merger, it had acquired the five thousand mile–long Chicago and North Western Railroad (CNW). Even though that earlier consolidation had big problems, top management ignored the early warning signs that the strategy was flawed, and used that same strategy to fold in the SP operations. The fact of poor implementation was not that hard to see. A veteran railroad observer, quoted in the *Wall Street Journal* just nine months before the SP merger, described the UP-CNW merger this way: "It has been about the ugliest operational situation I have seen since I have been around railroads."[14] In a pattern that would be repeated with the SP merger, UP did not listen to the locals when those people described what had worked for them.[15] For example, the Midwestern location of CNW meant that a sizeable portion of their business was grain shipments. To keep operations moving during harvest, CNW moved large quantities of grain to Gulf ports by barge. When UP took over the CNW, management abandoned this practice, used rail to move the grain to the Gulf, and promptly congested the rail lines. Shipments throughout the system were delayed and complaints soared. Ironically, in support of their application to acquire SP, UP executives argued that they had "learned a lot about how to do it right the next time" from their experience with CNW.[16] In an even stranger twist of logic, they also argued that their problems with CNW would be solved if they were allowed to merge with SP. This reasoning fairly reeks of potential for trouble to escalate.[17] Hence, there were early and ample signs that the UP did not understand either itself or its environment. And with less understanding, there should be more surprises and less adequate coping with any of them.

The more general point—and one that is crucial to those seeking effective ways of managing the unexpected—is that strategic goals contain a subtle trap. The trap is this. Strategic goals explicitly describe how the organization wants to position itself. But they do not describe the important mistakes people should guard against in pursuit of these goals.[18] It is the failure both to *articulate* important mistakes that must not occur and to *organize* in order to detect them that allows unexpected events to spin out of control. If an organization has an inflated view of its capability, there is little incentive to think about important mistakes simply because people assume there won't be any. A less charitable way to state this point is to say that arrogance and hubris breed vulnerability. UP, by many accounts, was the poster child of arrogance. This was true both internally, where its culture was described as militaristic and intimidating,[19] and externally, where shippers were given take-it-or-leave-it deals and where acquired railroads were viewed as inept.

What, then, would a less arrogant style of management look like? How do people act when they are mindful that important mistakes can scuttle the most luminous strategy? Those questions are the focus of this book. We draw our answers to those questions from a neglected body of work, namely, studies of organizations that operate under trying conditions yet have less than their fair share of accidents. Even though high reliability organizations such as aircraft carriers and nuclear power plants may seem unique, that impression is misleading. These organizations provide important lessons about managing the unexpected because of what they do on the input side, not because of what they generate on the output side. That people can be killed on an aircraft carrier but not at Silicon Graphics matters less than that people in both organizations make an effort on the input side to complicate rather than simplify their processes of attention. People who maintain complex sets of expectations (that is, have complicated mental models of how events unfold)[20] experience fewer unexpected events. And when unexpected events do occur, complex models enable people to "read" those anomalies earlier in their development and to re-solve them with smaller interventions. Those are the kinds of similarities we are after.

■ Hallmarks of High Reliability

In this book we focus on five hallmarks of organizations that persistently have less than their fair share of accidents. Together, these characteristics of HROs make up what we have termed *mindfulness*. They are

- Preoccupation with failure
- Reluctance to simplify interpretations
- Sensitivity to operations
- Commitment to resilience
- Deference to expertise

Here we briefly describe these key characteristics of high reliability organizations and how failures in these areas caused problems for Union Pacific.

Preoccupation with Failure

Even though high reliability organizations are noteworthy be-cause they avoid disasters, they do not gloat over this fact. Just the opposite. They are *preoccupied with their failures*, large and mostly small. They treat any lapse as a symptom that something is wrong with the system, something that could have severe con-sequences if separate small errors happen to coincide at one awful moment (for example, the disastrous release of poisonous chemicals from the Union Carbide plant in Bhopal, India, in 1984). HROs encourage reporting of errors, they elaborate ex-periences of a near miss for what can be learned, and they are

wary of the potential liabilities of success, including complacency, the temptation to reduce margins of safety, and the drift
into automatic processing.

Against this background what stands out about the Union
Pacific is its preoccupation with success and its denial of failures.
It is the classic case of top management being buffered from bad
news, a pattern that was repeated at all levels of the hierarchy.
For example, in November 1995, during the horrendous shipping delays of the CNW merger, then CEO and president Ron
Burns wrote a letter of apology to shippers. Burns, a nonrail-
roader (he came to UP from Enron in August 1995), was praised
by the shippers for this act, but he was also severely criticized
internally for his admission that UP had failed.[21] He lost his job
ten months after the letter was sent.[22] Persuaded by their own
rhetoric of competence that they had used in Washington to influence regulators, UP executives neither looked for failures nor
believed that they would find many if they did. This message
was not lost on those at the operating level. As a result, slow-
downs were underreported and allowed to incubate until they
were undeniable and close to irreversible.

Reluctance to Simplify

Another way HROs manage for the unexpected is by being *reluctant to accept simplifications*. Success in any coordinated activity requires that people simplify in order to stay focused on
a handful of key issues and key indicators. HROs take deliberate steps to create more complete and nuanced pictures. They
simplify less and see more. Knowing that the world they face is
complex, unstable, unknowable, and unpredictable, they position themselves to see as much as possible. They encourage
boundary spanners who have diverse experience, skepticism
toward received wisdom, and negotiating tactics that reconcile

differences of opinion without destroying the nuances that diverse people detect.

Union Pacific presents a somewhat different picture. UP has a dominant logic that simplifies how railroads work. Trains are made up in central locations called classification yards, not in dispersed locations called shipper yards, satellite yards, or mainline tracks. Freight shipped by railroaders is moved by rail, not barge. The problems caused by these simplifications are overlooked until the central location or excessive grain shipments become a bottleneck. Simplification, in the case of UP, is encouraged by the preference for staffing top management positions with railroad people. Some of the more innovative moves at UP were made by outsider Michael Walsh, who was chairman and CEO of the railroad in the late 1980s. In fact, Walsh's innovations were featured in a Tom Peters documentary about how the tradition-bound railroad industry finally found its way into the twentieth century. Walsh's era was not a popular period for veteran railroaders. And when Walsh moved on to Tenneco, Davidson assumed the CEO portion of Walsh's job, while Drew Lewis assumed the chairman's duties.[23] Both these moves ensured that UP was once more back in the hands of insiders. The subsequent short interval during which outsider Ron Burns attempted to run a more customer-focused railroad only served to confirm the belief that the Union Pacific was in the best hands if those hands belonged to veteran railroaders. That belief is understandable. It makes for a cohesive top management team. But that team is of one mind simply because the minds that compose it are redundant. Everyone sees the same warning signals and is blind to the same unexpected warnings. That kind of homogeneity can encourage people, under the guise of consensus, to misread local innovations and workarounds as signs of inefficiency rather than as adaptations that make the difference between profit and loss.

Sensitivity to Operations

An additional characteristic of HROs, *sensitivity to operations*, points to their ongoing concern with the unexpected. Unexpected events usually originate in what psychologist James Reason calls "latent failures." Latent failures are "loopholes in the system's defenses, barriers and safeguards whose potential existed for some time prior to the onset of the accident sequence, though usually without any obvious bad effect."[24] These loopholes consist of imperfections in features such as supervision, reporting of defects, engineered safety procedures, safety training, briefings, certification, and hazard identification. Many of these latent failures are discovered only after the fact of an accident. But that need not be the case. Normal operations may reveal deficiencies that are "free lessons" that signal the development of unexpected events. But these lessons are visible only if there is frequent assessment of the overall safety health of the organization.

This is an area where HROs distinguish themselves. They are attentive to the front line, where the real work gets done. The "big picture" in HROs is less strategic and more situational than is true of most other organizations. When people have well-developed situational awareness, they can make the continuous adjustments that prevent errors from accumulating and enlarging. Anomalies are noticed while they are still tractable and can still be isolated. All this is made possible because HROs are aware of the close tie between sensitivity to operations and sensitivity to relationships. People who refuse to speak up out of fear enact a system that knows less than it needs to know to remain effective. People in HROs know that you can't develop a big picture of operations if the symptoms of those operations are withheld. It makes no difference whether they are withheld out of fear, ignorance, or indifference. All those reasons for withholding are relational. If managers refuse to examine what happens between heads, they'll be eternally puzzled by what appears to happen inside individual heads.

In contrast, there is general agreement that relationships at the UP were tense. People keep mentioning intimidation, a militaristic culture, hollow promises to customers, abandonment of workarounds, production pressure on train crews, and the same old resources thrown at problems (for example, send more engines to an already immobilized rail yard). What is striking is the disconnect between operations as viewed at the top and operations as implemented on the front line. Theoretically, the language of operations should have been a common language at UP that everyone from top to bottom could understand and use to resolve merger-related problems. Practically, that didn't happen. At the top, "sensitivity to operations" meant improving the balance sheet and sensitivity to escalating costs (for example, overtime). At the bottom, "sensitivity to operations" meant sensitivity to the fact that trains were backing up outside the Englewood yard and that the entire UP system was grinding to a halt. Hence, there were at least two "big pictures" of operations at UP, not one.

Commitment to Resilience

No system is perfect. HROs know this as well as anyone. This is why they complement their anticipatory activities of learning from failures, complicating their perceptions, and remaining sensitive to operations with a *commitment to resilience*. HROs develop capabilities to detect, contain, and bounce back from those inevitable errors that are part of an indeterminate world.[25] The signature of an HRO is not that it is error-free, but that errors don't disable it.

Resilience is a combination of keeping errors small and of improvising workarounds that keep the system functioning.

Both these avenues of resilience demand deep knowledge of the technology, the system, one's coworkers, one's self, and the raw materials. HROs put a premium on experts; personnel with deep experience, skills of recombination, and training. They mentally simulate worst case conditions and practice their own equivalent of fire drills. Psychologist Gary Klein, an expert in high-stakes decision making, suggests that the most effective fire commanders have rich fantasy lives and mentally simulate potential lines of attack.

The meltdown of operations at UP by definition shows an inability to bounce back. When some trains began to back up, even more trains began to back up. The problem got worse, not better. There is little evidence of learning, either from the CNW merger or from the massive backups that had occurred years before in the Conrail consolidation. There is little evidence of resilient improvisation to deal with the unexpected. The UP remained essentially a by-the-books operator that favored centralization and formalization and treated improvisation as insubordination.[26] People who bypassed the hierarchical decision structure and enacted unique solutions not prescribed in existing procedures were accused of being insubordinate. In addition, there is little evidence that slack resources were reallocated, a common way to create resilience. The UP trimmed crews, locomotives, and supervisors shortly before the Englewood disaster and removed whatever slack they had. A more subtle loss of resilience occurred when UP argued that the merger had merit because the SP was in terrible shape and only the UP could save it. That reasoning is dangerous because, once the merger was approved, UP had to run twice as much railroad with basically the same resources as before. Management couldn't very well merge the companies and then delegate key operations to people they had just labeled inept. In short, most of the moves made by the UP removed rather than added resilience.

Deference to Expertise

The final distinctive feature of HROs is their *deference to expertise.* HROs cultivate diversity, not just because it helps them notice more in complex environments, but also because it helps them do more with the complexities they spot. Rigid hierarchies have their own special vulnerability to error. Errors at higher levels tend to pick up and combine with errors at lower levels, thereby making the resulting problem bigger, harder to comprehend, and more prone to escalation. To prevent this deadly scenario, HROs push decision making down—and around. Decisions are made on the front line, and authority migrates to the people with the most expertise, regardless of their rank. This is not simply a case of people deferring to the person with the "most experience." Experience by itself is no guarantee of expertise, since all too often people have the same experience over and over and do little to elaborate those repetitions. The pattern of decisions "migrating" to expertise is found in flight operations on aircraft carriers, where "uniqueness coupled with the need for accurate decisions leads to decisions that 'search' for the expert and migrate around the organization. The decisions migrate around these organizations in search of a person who has specific knowledge of the event. This person may be someone who has a longer tenure on the carrier or in the specific job."[27]

At the UP, however, decisions were made at the top and continued to be made this way regardless of whether they were made during times of crisis or times of calm. This meant that decisions about the Englewood yard were being made by an overloaded team of people who were not current in their operational skills and who were being fed information they wanted to hear. Davidson kept saying publicly that the worst was over when, in fact, the worst was yet to come. He kept sending UP people to see what was up rather than going himself to observe this firsthand or listening to Southern Pacific experts who had run the yards successfully. This is the classic command-and-control bureaucracy that is adequate for a stable world but too inflexible in times of change.

HROs differentiate between normal times, high-tempo times, and emergencies and clearly signal which mode they are operating in. Decisions come from the top when it is normal, they migrate during high-tempo operations, and a predefined emergency structure kicks in when there is danger the ship could be lost. These clear signals tell everyone when migration is crucial and when it is not. No such signals were available at the UP. There was no agreed-upon way to signal, systemwide, either that this was a unique period with unusual pressure and problems or that "we are in big trouble." Crisis times were treated just like normal times. As a result, people did what they always did, only they did more of it. So when the system approached gridlock, more people and more equipment were thrown at the problem. What top people did not do was consult different resources, listen, pull cars out of the system, bypass the system, rebuild a system elsewhere, or own up to the growing calamity. Stonewalling does not manage the unexpected. HROs have learned this lesson the hard way.

■ What Can We Learn from Those Who Face Catastrophes?

Part of the novelty of the argument presented in this book is that we have taken a persistent pressing problem—*How can we manage the unexpected?*—and suggested a new answer: *By acting more like a high reliability organization.* These high reliability organizations maintain reliable performance despite constant exposure to the unexpected, in part by developing and maintaining their capability for mindfulness. A well-developed capability for mindfulness catches the unexpected earlier, when it is smaller, comprehends its potential importance despite the small size of the disruption, and removes, contains, or rebounds from the effects of the unexpected. By managing the unexpected mindfully, HROs continue to deliver reliably the performance they were chartered to deliver.

Issues of Harm

HROs have a big incentive to contain the unexpected because when they fail to do so, the results can be catastrophic. Lives can be lost, but so can assets, careers, reputations, legitimacy, credibility, support, trust, and goodwill. All organizations know firsthand the potential for the latter losses. It is the very fact of these high stakes in HROs that makes them unusually good models of how to handle the unexpected. Yet in the eyes of many observers, these high stakes may make HROs seem irrelevant. Without giving the matter much thought, some people tend to dismiss the relevance of HROs to their own activities with the pat remark, "We don't kill people. What can we learn from those who live in chronic fear that they might?"

If you think about it, that reaction doesn't make much sense. If people are serious about becoming a "learning organization," they should not impose strict definitions in advance about where the learning will come from. The whole point of a learning organization is that it needs to get a better handle on the fact that it doesn't know what it doesn't know.

It is commonplace among people in business to claim that "it's a jungle out there," meaning that the world is filled with physical, financial, and psychological casualties. True, most of us don't see ourselves as working in places that kill people. Neither do most people who work in HROs. There were no fatalities at the Three Mile Island nuclear power accident, even though much hand wringing implies there were. In fact, the consequences of a lack of mindfulness in business can be no less deadly than in HROs. Deck operations on carriers kill fewer people in a year than died at the Union Pacific the year it tried to absorb Southern Pacific. To the currently controversial question of how many people die each year from medical errors, the answers range as high as the equivalent of two fully loaded 747s crashing with no survivors, each day of the year. Hospitals aren't even considered high reliability organizations. The existence of any pattern in these statistics is not obvious. And that's the point. The ability of HROs to teach us about mindfulness does not lie in their outcomes, or in the noncomparability of their outcomes with yours. It lies instead on the input side: what they pay attention to, how they process it, and how they struggle to maintain continuing alertness.

HROs, in fact, are organizations like any other. All organizations, HROs and businesses alike, develop culturally accepted beliefs about the world and its hazards. All organizations develop precautionary norms that are set out in regulations, procedures, rules, guidelines, job descriptions, and training materials, as well as informally on the grapevine. And all organizations accumulate unnoticed events that are at odds with accepted beliefs about hazards and norms for avoiding these hazards.[28] It is these very similarities that encourage transfer of the lessons of HROs to other organizations. For example, HROs develop beliefs about the world and its hazards with fewer simplifications, less finality, and with more revision than we see in most organizations. The definition of what is hazardous is continually refreshed. Likewise, HROs develop precautionary norms just like everyone else. But unlike everyone else, they use both the small failures and liabilities of success as sources for these precautions. And like all organizations, HROs accumulate unnoticed events that are at odds with what they expected, but they tend to notice these accumulated events sooner, when they are smaller in size. They also concentrate more fully on the discrepancy, its meaning, and its most decisive resolution. Each of these elaborations of the basics by HROs suggests directions in which other organizations can make their own elaborations in the interest of heightened mindfulness.

Issues of Scale

Another source of misunderstanding about the relevance of HROs to non-HROs involves a misunderstanding of issues of scale. If the activity being observed is an assembly line, for example, an unexpected shutdown is not a severe crisis (there was no fatality). But it is a crisis relative to what the supervisor expected would not fail and a crisis relative to precautions taken so that it wouldn't fail. A visit from Mike Wallace to a CEO's office does not produce fatalities, but it can affect markets, share price, and liability. In each case the meaning of the unexpected is contextual. Once we understand the context, the precautions, the assumptions, the focus of attention, and what was ignored, it becomes clear that many organizations are just as exposed to threats as are HROs, and just as much in need of mindfulness. In all organizations people do things that they expect to continue doing reliably and for which unexpected interruptions can eventually turn disastrous if they manage the unexpected poorly. This possibility is more at the center of attention for HROs than for most other organizations. But it is a possibility that haunts all organizations.

As noted earlier, how well or poorly people manage the unexpected is a foundational issue that underlies the handling of any pressing business problem. Hence, the difference between an HRO and a non-HRO is not as large as it might appear. In both settings, trouble starts small and is signaled by weak symptoms that are easy to miss, especially when expectations are strong and mindfulness is weak. These small discrepancies can cumulate, enlarge, and have disproportionately large consequences. This path of development also is similar across organizations. What differ across organizations are variables such as how much value people place on catching such developments earlier rather than later, how much knowledge people have of the system and its capacity to detect and remedy early indications of trouble, and how much support there is from top management to allocate resources to early detection and management of the unexpected, error-acknowledging communication, and commitment to mindfulness at all levels.

Issues of the Setting

The environment of HROs is one in which there are high-risk technologies. These technologies must be mastered by means other than trial-and-error learning, since in many cases the first error will also be the last trial. HRO environments unfold rapidly and errors propagate quickly. Understanding is never perfect, and people are under pressure to make wise choices with insufficient information. But whose environment isn't like this? Stanford business professor Kathleen Eisenhardt, for example, describes the environments of the microcomputer industry as "high velocity environments." "High velocity environments are characterized by rapid and discontinuous change in demand, competitors, technology, and/or regulation such that information is often inaccurate, unavailable, or obsolete."[29] The ways people deal with a high-velocity environment resemble the mindful activities of people in HROs. For example, she finds that her fast decision makers pay close attention to "real-time information, that is, information about current operations or the current environment which is reported with little or no time lag."[30] The parallel to our third process of mindfulness, *sensitivity to operations*, is clear. Eisenhardt also finds simultaneous centralization-decentralization, which we describe in Chapter Five under How Culture Controls, to be a signature of HROs. She finds it in the form of a pattern she calls "consensus with qualification," which refers to a two-step decision process. The first step is decentralized because everyone who will be affected by the decision tries to reach a consensus on what it should be. But if they can't reach it, the decision is made in a centralized fashion by the leader.

In summary, HROs worry about the unexpected, mindfulness, and reliability, but so do an increasing number of organizations. The UP is not alone in its troubles with the unexpected. E-commerce, new economic rules, offshore manufacturing, constantly changing parent companies, and jolts of downsizing put every organization in the same position as the UP. Everyone has their own Englewood yard, patched together with baling wire and duct tape, which is just itching to spring the unexpected. For people who hate surprises, a stream of unexpected events can be a pressing problem. It is a problem whose resolution lies partly in the lessons learned by those who live with a steady diet of the unexpected.

CHAPTER SUMMARY

In this chapter we have introduced the topic of *managing the unexpected* by looking at the efforts of the Union Pacific Railroad to absorb both the Chicago and North Western Railroad and the Southern Pacific Railroad in the short span of two years. Both mergers generated escalating events that paralyzed the UP system. These difficulties can be viewed as problems in managing the unexpected. The UP was not prepared for the unexpected. Its management team dealt with it poorly as it unfolded. And when they tried to bounce back from the unexpected, they often made things worse.

A benchmark for best practices in managing the unexpected is a set of organizations, called high reliability organizations, that reliably forestall catastrophic outcomes through mindful attention to ongoing operations. People in these organizations hate the unexpected just as much as everyone else. But it doesn't surprise them or disable them. And their coping actions seldom make the situation worse.

We have summarized five ways in which HROs operate that make them more aware of their own capabilities, what they face, and what it might mean: preoccupation with failure, reluctance to simplify interpretations, sensitivity to operations, commitment to resilience, and deference to expertise. These guidelines apply upward to divisions and organizations as well as downward to teams, crews, and team leaders. Although HROs seem unlike any other organization, that appearance is deceptive. They resemble other organizations in their input processes, their adoption of precautionary beliefs, and their susceptibility to surprises. Where they differ is in their commitment to mindfulness as a means to manage inputs, precautions, and surprises. Even though HROs may be unique in their pursuit of mindfulness, there is nothing unique about how they pursue it. Processes by which HROs pursue mindfulness are processes that can be adopted by anyone. The purpose of this book is to make those processes more visible, accessible, and available.

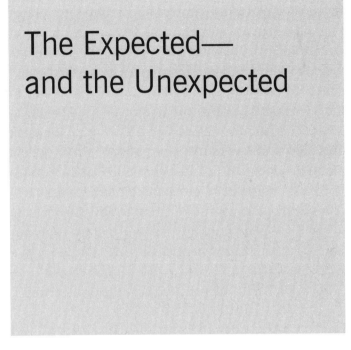

The Expected—
and the Unexpected

mong the most attentive and mindful people in the world
are those who cycle between action and interpretation on
nuclear aircraft carriers. These people have to be mindful
or they can get killed. People who work on carriers spend much
of their time on a flat deck that has been called "the most dangerous four and one-half acres in the world." This "acreage" is
filled with up to eighty jet aircraft, some of which at any one time
are being fueled with their engines running, or having armed
lethal weapons attached to their wings, or being launched off the
front of the ship by two million horsepower catapults that accelerate the 65,000 pound plane to 150 miles per hour in three
seconds, or are being recovered simultaneously at the back end

of the ship by what amounts to a "controlled crash." When a plane lands, a tailhook on the aircraft is supposed to catch one of four arresting wires that are strung across the landing area and bring the aircraft to an abrupt stop. To call the stop "abrupt" is an understatement, since the aircraft's engines are pushed to full power the moment the plane hits the deck just in case it fails to snag any of the wires and has to go around for a second try. Without full power, the plane could dribble off the end of the deck and crash into the ocean. As if this were not enough for people to worry about, the deck is often slippery with a mixture of sea water and oil, blasts from jet engines and afterburners leave few safe places to stand, vocal communication is difficult, and the people who run these operations are nineteen and twenty-year-old kids, many of whom had never before seen a jet close-up, a ship, or the ocean.

Here's how one Navy veteran describes life on a carrier:

> Imagine that it's a busy day, and you shrink San Francisco airport to only one short runway and one ramp and one gate. Make planes take off and land at the same time, at half the present time interval, rock the runway from side to side, and require that everyone who leaves in the morning returns the same day. Make sure the equipment is so close to the envelope that it's fragile. Then turn off the radar to avoid detection, impose strict controls on the radios, fuel the aircraft in place with their engines running, put an enemy in the air, and scatter live bombs and rockets around. Now wet the whole thing down with sea water and oil, and man it with twenty-year-olds, half of whom have never seen an airplane close-up. Oh, and by the way, try not to kill anyone.[1]

Can you think of another environment that is quite this full of the unexpected? Can you think of a better group than a carrier to use as a benchmark for your own efforts to be more alert, mindful, resilient? Can you imagine how dangerous a carrier would be if the Union Pacific's management team were in charge and calling the shots the same way they did at Englewood? But can you also see how your own management team at times behaves like the UP team? Carriers may seem a lot different from the organizations you know well, but carriers confront and solve many of the same problems you face. The difference is, people on carriers can't afford to be wrong. And you can. Or at least you think you can. What most managers keep forgetting, and what carriers seldom forget, is that small moments of inattention and misperception can escalate swiftly into unmanageable trouble. If you pay close attention to how people manage the unexpected on carriers, you'll learn ways to improve your own effectiveness in dealing with the unexpected (on land).

The purpose of this chapter is to show why the ideas of the expected, the unexpected, and mindfulness are so crucial to effective performance. We illustrate this importance using examples from one kind of high reliability organization, a nuclear aircraft carrier.[2] First, we give a flavor of deck operations on a carrier so that you can visualize key activities. Then we explore the ideas of the expected and the unexpected, with special attention to the unexpected and the surprising. We then introduce the idea of mindfulness in more detail and show how it handles flaws in expectations, helps people understand and cope with the unexpected, and improves system functioning. We conclude by summarizing the main argument.

■ Reliable Flight Operations on a Carrier

The potential for trouble on a carrier cannot be overemphasized. It is not just that you have six thousand people crammed into tight spaces away from shore on an 1,100 foot, 95,000-ton floating city run by an overburdened "mayor." Within those tight spaces on a carrier you also have people working with jet aircraft,

jet fuel, nuclear reactors, nuclear weapons, an onboard air traffic control system, refueling and resupply from adjacent ships
that are moving, a surrounding battle group of seven to nine
ships that are supposed to protect the carrier but that can themselves also be dangerous obstacles in fog or high seas, and unpredictable weather. The list of "gee whiz" stuff on a carrier
seems endless.

Flight Operations and Medical Treatment

What is surprising is the extent to which the qualities of a well-
functioning carrier generalize to other organizations. This is evident, for example, in recent discussions of medical errors that
suggest close parallels between health care systems and the systems that contribute to effectiveness in carriers. For example, the
influential report on medical errors developed by the Institute
of Medicine had this to say: Health care

> is very different from a manufacturing process, mostly because
> of huge variability in patients and circumstances, the need to
> adapt processes quickly, the rapidly changing knowledge base,
> and the importance of highly trained professionals who must
> use expert judgment in dynamic settings. . . .[T]he performance
> of crews and flight personnel on aircraft carriers provides an
> example that has features that are closer to those in health care
> environments than manufacturing. On an aircraft carrier, fuel-
> ing aircraft and loading munitions are examples of the risks
> posed when performing incompatible activities in close prox-
> imity. On the flight deck, 100 to 200 people fuel, load muni-
> tions, and maintain aircraft that take off and are recovered at
> 48 to 60-second intervals. . . . [These flight operations are] an
> example of organizational performance requiring nearly con-
> tinuous operational reliability despite complex interrelated
> patterns among many people. These activities cannot be fully
> mapped out beforehand because of changes in weather (e.g.

wind direction and strength), sea conditions, time of day and visibility, returning aircraft arrivals, and so forth. Yet, surprisingly, generally mapped out sequences can be carried out with very high reliability in novel situations using improvisation and adaptation and personnel who are highly trained but not highly educated. . . . As in health care, it is not possible in such dynamic settings to anticipate and write a rule for every circumstance. Once-rigid orders that prescribed how to perform each operation have been replaced by more flexible, less hierarchical methods. For example, although the captain's commands usually take precedence, junior officers can, and do, change these priorities when they believe that following an order will risk the crew's safety. Such an example demonstrates that even in technologically sophisticated, hazardous, and unpredictable environments it is possible to foster real-time problem solving and to institute safety systems that incorporate a knowledge of human factors.[3]

Flight Operations and Your Firm

Although the scale of all this is awesome, the problems of a carrier are actually no different from the problems you face. The basic task of people on a carrier is to move aircraft off the pointed end of the ship and back onto the blunt end of the ship. Your basic task is to move products or services out the front door and raw materials in the back door. Carrier personnel have to transform the raw materials of new recruits, fickle technology, and unreliable aircraft into total readiness, just as you have to transform your raw materials into something that is better than what your competitors have to offer. Carrier personnel add value and achieve victory. You add value and achieve sales. Carriers have to live within budgets and so do you. On carriers, budgets for aviation fuel are sometimes cut, with the result that pilots literally get less practice at difficult night landings than they should, which can cause serious trouble down the line.

Pleas from the captain through the chain of command to the very top, the joint chiefs, do not necessarily bring relief. And your pleas often meet a similar fate. People on carriers pay close attention to how often pilots achieve their goal of a perfect landing and snag the third arresting wire with their tailhook. Less perfect, more dangerous landings occur when the pilot snags the first wire (the aircraft is closer to crashing into the stern of the vessel) or the fourth wire (the aircraft is close to failing to achieve flying speed and falling into the ocean). By comparison, you pay attention to very different standards to measure performance, standards such as inventory turn, sales booked at the end of the quarter, volume of customer complaints. Your world and the world of a carrier look very different. And yet both of you are trying to gauge the health of your systems. Both of you are trying to discover clear criteria of performance, while you also try to remain alert, avoid complacence, learn from failures, and cope with whatever is thrown at you.

The captain is held responsible for a safe ship, but production pressures squeeze the time and resources available to him to ensure safety. You, too, are held responsible for execution without significant mistakes, but time and resources to do so are often in short supply for you as well. People on carriers worry a lot about safety. But you have similar concerns. You worry about reducing risks, maintaining dependable procedures, meeting irrevocable deadlines, protecting your activities from harm, being less exposed and vulnerable, and working with more security. Those are issues of safety. They are issues of reliability. They are issues you face in common with the captain of a carrier.

There is a peculiar property of safety that makes it hard to talk about and hard to achieve for both of you. Safety is elusive because "it is a dynamic non-event—what produces the stable outcome is constant change rather than continuous repetition. To achieve this stability, a change in one system parameter must be compensated for by change in other parameters."[4] The problem is that when a system is operating safely and reliably there are constant outcomes and nothing to pay attention to. That does not mean that nothing is happening, even though it is tempting to draw that conclusion. Quite the opposite. There is continuous *mutual* adjustment. One change is compensated for by another change. The deck becomes more slippery so the spacing between the planes is increased. The radio signal begins to break up so the crew resorts to hand signals. The seas get heavy so aircraft are not moved between decks on elevators that are exposed to the sea. Armed weapons explode at different temperatures so one person is removed from deck duty and assigned the sole task of recording which weapons are on which planes. In the event of a deck fire, fire fighters will know which areas need immediate attention to prevent explosion.

Mutual adjustments like this preserve reliability and are accomplished only through a combination of respectful interaction, communication, trust, firsthand knowledge of the technology, attentiveness, familiarity with one another's roles, and experience.[5] This combination of capabilities enables people to deal with dynamic nonevents, and to keep the unexpected as a nonevent.

Flight Operations and Expectations

Expectations and mindfulness hold people and activities together on carriers, just as they do in other HROs. Here's an example of how that works, taken from Gene Rochlin's fieldnotes on board the carrier *Carl Vinson:*

> Almost everyone involved in bringing aircraft on board is part of one of several constant loops of conversation and verification, taking place over several different channels at once. At first, little of this chatter seems coherent, let alone substantive, to the outside observer. With experience, one discovers that

seasoned personnel do not "listen" so much as they monitor for deviation, reacting almost instantaneously to anything that does not fit their expectations of the correct routine. This constant flow of information about each safety-critical activity is designed specifically to assure that any critical element that is out of place will be discovered or noticed by someone before it causes problems.[6]

Rochlin's example is a compact summary of how expectations and mindfulness work together. Continuous talk sets up expectations. These expectations enable people to spot failures, hear the unexpected, maintain the big picture of operations involving several simultaneous conversations, see what needs attention, and infer who needs to make the relevant decision. Expectations are the threads that link these conversations. Disconfirmations are the breaks in those conversations that signal early signs of trouble. These breaks, or as Rochlin calls them, "anything that does not fit," are the small incidents that can be managed earlier with less disruption. Those same breaks can also be ignored. But if they are ignored, they often enlarge and cause even more disruption. Early detection as well as early management keeps the disruption from turning into a pressing problem. That is true for carriers. It is true for medical treatment teams. It is true for HROs in general. And it is probably true for your organization.

The elements that produce safety on a carrier are quite straightforward. They include communication, respectful interaction, and competence in filling one's role and performing the tasks associated with that role. What is unique about carriers and other HROs is that they do these things mindfully in the belief that safety is not bankable.[7] HROs are clear that you can't "fix" the safety problem, store up safety, and then move on to something else. If the people on a carrier have been failure free for sixty-seven days, that does not mean that their system is safe.

And it does not mean that their attention and effort can be relaxed. Instead, all it means is that the unexpected has not yet escaped containment. But it could at any moment, especially if mutual adjustments are not continued. Safety and reliability have to be re-accomplished over and over. Remember, safety and reliability are *dynamic* nonevents. They are not static nonevents. Safety and reliability are complex outcomes that require continuous attention and effort. Anything that might affect that attention and effort adversely is of vital interest for anyone who wants to produce sustained high performance. Just such an influence is the set of expectations that people use to guide their efforts. Expectations matter when it comes to safety and reliability because they can have an adverse effect. The following discussion shows how expectations can sometimes lead to adversity and what can be done to forestall that outcome.

■ Expectations

There is no great mystery about what an expectation is.[8] To have an expectation is to envision something, usually for good reasons, that is reasonably certain to come about. To expect something is to be mentally ready for it. Every deliberate action you take is based on assumptions about how the world will react to what you do. "Expectancies form the basis for virtually all deliberate actions because expectancies about how the world operates serve as implicit assumptions that guide behavioral choices."[9, 10] Expectations provide a significant infrastructure for everyday life. They are like a planning function that suggests the likely course of events. Expectations direct your attention to certain features of events, which means that they affect what you notice, mull over, and remember. When you expect that something will happen, that is a lot like testing a hypothesis. For example, if you expect that a bolt left on a carrier deck is no big deal, that's a hypothesis. If the bolt is ingested into a jet engine, and if the engine explodes (which has actually happened during carrier deployments), you are wrong, the expectation is disconfirmed, and you and your system have learned a lesson the hard way. In fact, carriers conduct foreign object damage (FOD) walkdowns several times a day to prevent just such a calamity.[11] Everyone together, regardless of rank, walks the full length of the deck and picks up anything that might be sucked into an engine. The FOD walkdown is a microcosm of how expectations function, how they can produce blind spots, and how their disconfirmation can be the basis for both serious problems and learning.

The Search for Confirmation

Most of your expectations are reasonably accurate and tend to be confirmed, partly because they are based on your experience and partly because you correct faulty assumptions whenever they have negative consequences. The tricky part is that all of us tend to be awfully generous in what we treat as evidence that our expectations are confirmed.[12] Furthermore, we actively seek out evidence that confirms our expectations and avoid evidence that disconfirms them. For example, if you expect that Navy aviators are brash, you'll tend to do a one-sided search for indications of brashness whenever you spot an aviator.[13] You're less likely to do a more balanced search where you weigh all the evidence and look just as closely for disconfirming evidence in the form of tentative, modest behavior. This lopsided search sets at least two problems in motion. First, you overlook accumulating evidence that events are not developing as you thought they would. And second, you tend to overestimate the validity of those expectations you now hold. Both tendencies become even stronger if you are overloaded and under pressure. As pressure increases people are more likely to search for confirming information and to ignore information that is inconsistent with their expectations.

People in HROs work hard to counteract this tendency. They routinely suspect that their expectations are incomplete, and that they can come closer to having it right if they doubt the very expectations that have been confirmed most often. For example, landing signal officers, who guide pilots onto the carrier deck in their last few seconds of flight, assume that pilots are coolheaded, not prone to panic, and wouldn't even be flying onto a carrier if the opposite were true. And yet these officers also know that seasoned pilots can sometimes panic when, for example, they get disoriented at night, can't distinguish between the black sky and the black sea, and unexpectedly lose altitude while circling to dump excess fuel. If landing officers expect that a pilot is calm, they often listen even more closely to the quality of his or her voice to detect subtle cues of tension that suggest the expectation is wrong and that this particular nighttime recovery is going sour.

The tendency to seek confirmation and shun disconfirmation is a well-honed, well-practiced human tendency. That's why HROs have to work so hard and so continuously to override this tendency and remain alert. And that's why you may have to work just as hard. All of us face an ongoing *struggle* for alertness because we face an ongoing preference for information that confirms.

The Unexpected

Managing the unexpected is about alertness, sensemaking, updating, and staying in motion. But it all starts with a simple, straightforward, common sequence in organizational life that we mentioned in Chapter One: A person or unit has an intention, takes action, misunderstands the world; actual events fail to coincide with the intended sequence; and there is an unexpected outcome.[14]

Varieties of Surprise

Surprises and the unexpected come in many forms. Strategy researcher Brian Kylen has suggested that surprise and the unexpected can take at least five forms.[15] First, surprise can take the form of what he calls "a bolt from the blue." Something appears for which you had no expectation, no prior model of the event, no hint that it was coming. In the case of carriers, an example of a bolt from the blue would be the addition of women pilots to crews that had been an all-male stronghold for decades. No one expected this and it made no sense. Federal law precluded women from flying combat missions, there was no improvement in readiness or economic advantage gained by assigning the small number of women jet pilots to extended cruises, women pilots had not previously been trained to deploy in fleet squadrons, there were few women qualified to fly off ships, and the casual atmosphere of the ready room on the ship sometimes led to more tension in crew relationships when women used the same facilities. Against this background, the jolt of surprise felt when a plane landed on the deck and a woman pilot stepped out is hard to overestimate.

A second form of surprise occurs when an issue is recognized but the direction of the expectation is wrong. For example, fatigue is an issue on carriers and everyone recognizes it. It is not uncommon during high-tempo periods for people to be on for twenty hours, off for four, and back on for twenty. The expectation is that fatigued crews will perform more poorly than fresh crews. The surprise in all of this is that in many cases, the opposite happens. Fatigued crews have worked together, know each other's quirks, accommodate them, and perform well as a unit. Fresh crews, people who are relative strangers to one another, often have to work out their coordination and rhythms and are rusty at the beginning of their shift. It takes time to develop smooth coordination, so performance is below average early in the shift and gets better as the shift progresses.

A third form of surprise occurs when you know what will happen, when it will happen, and in what order, but you discover that your timing is off. On carriers that are deployed for a period of eight months, there is the expectation that as the cruise progresses and reaches perhaps the six-month mark, morale will sag, people will start to feel closed in, tempers will get a little shorter, and exchanges will be a little more prickly. This expectation can turn into a surprise when all these actions occur much earlier, say, just two months into an eight-month cruise. Since this problem occurs much earlier than expected, the chances are good that there were clues that tensions were higher than usual, but they were missed and coded instead as "normal" trouble of people settling in for a long cruise.

A fourth form of surprise occurs when the expected duration of an event proves to be wrong. An event whose effect was expected to be transient turns out to have an enduring effect. On carriers, at the beginning of a cruise, when people are still unfamiliar with their tasks and each other, coordination is clumsy, communication is uneven, and the ship is less safe than the captain wants. (This same pattern also appears at the end of the cruise when people are eager to get home and may overlook unsafe conditions whose correction would delay disembarkation.) Surprise occurs when an expectation that poor coordination will be transient proves false, and the poor coordination persists. The captain's continuing belief that the coordination will improve and that improvement is taking "just a little longer than usual" can be deadly if bad habits are being learned, people are growing more and more reluctant to speak up, and the poor performance becomes something that is no longer discussible. Surprises of duration are old hat to people who try to fathom business cycles. These people often find their "bullish" or "bearish" expectations dashed by "uncooperative" markets. Notice that investors seldom change their expectations. Instead, they talk about "aberrations," "imperfections," "misleading signals," and "corrections" in the markets. These attributions enable them to maintain their original expectation unchanged. That's no different from a commanding officer saying, "I see no reason to change my expectation that this crew will get its act together, even though it is taking a little longer than usual."

A fifth form of surprise occurs when a problem is expected but its amplitude is not. For example, it is expected that occasionally pilots will miss the arresting wires when they try to land on a carrier deck (this is called a *bolter*). When a pilot bolters, this interrupts the smooth functioning of the system while that person circles around for a second and sometimes a third try. It would be a surprise in amplitude if several people boltered on the same day or if several people in the same squadron did so. It would be a lot harder to blame a cluster of boltering on simple operator error. The alternative diagnosis of system error is more troubling and a much bigger threat to the captain's bottom line of full readiness to engage the enemy. A different example of an amplitude surprise involves the performance appraisal of a commanding officer. This appraisal often includes how successful that person has been in persuading members of the crew to reenlist when their tour of duty is finished. Typically some members are persuaded, and appraisers expect that this will be true for any commanding officer. But if not a single member of that officer's crew reenlisted, this would be a surprise of amplitude.

In each of these five cases, the surprise starts with an expectation. People start with expectations that aircraft carriers are ships manned by men, fatigue reduces coordination, resentment builds up when people are housed together in close quarters for long periods, coordination improves with time, and participation in high-risk activities is attractive to young men and women. Presumably, if you hold these expectations, you look for evidence that confirms them rather than evidence that disconfirms them. If you find confirming evidence, this "proves" that your hunches about the world are accurate, that you are in control, that you know what's up, and that you are safe. The continuing search for confirming evidence postpones your realization that something unexpected is developing. If you are slow to realize that things are not the way you expected them to be, the problem worsens and becomes harder to solve and gets entangled with other problems. When it finally becomes clear that your expectation is wrong, there may be few options left to resolve the problem. In the meantime, efficiency and effectiveness have declined, the system is now vulnerable to further collapse, and safety and reputations and production are on the line.

Dynamics of Surprise

Evidence shows that when something unexpected happens, this is an unpleasant experience. Part of managing the unexpected involves anticipating these feelings of unpleasantness and taking steps to minimize their impact. A surprise tends to be unpleasant because your world seems to be less predictable and less controllable than you first thought, and because you may feel committed to the predictions you make. When the unexpected happens, people pay closer attention to information related to the disconfirmed expectation and try to make sense of it. Strong feelings can distort this processing by leading people to use too little of the information that is potentially available to them. You probably know this form of distortion by the name *tunnel vision*. For example, if air traffic controllers are controlling traffic on a radar screen, and if pilots fail to execute their instructions in expected ways, the controllers sometimes narrow down their attention to just those portions where the unexpected has occurred. They neglect the activity of aircraft that are moving in other sectors of the screen, away from the small spot that has drawn all of their attention. When the controller's peripheral vision is reduced, serious problems can develop in the portions of the screen that are unmonitored.

When people pay closer attention to the circumstances surrounding a disconfirmed expectation, they often try to preserve
the original expectations by explaining away the disconfirmation.
For example, sociologist Diane Vaughan found this tendency to
normalize the unexpected in her re-analysis of the *Challenger* disaster. When unexpected burns appeared on the O-rings that
sealed sections of the booster rockets, engineers enlarged their
definition of what was an "acceptable risk" to include these indications that hot gases were leaking past the gaskets. What they
first treated as an unexpected anomaly was later redefined and
treated as an expected event. The range of expected error enlarged from the judgment that it was normal to have heat on the
primary O-ring, to normal to have erosion on the primary O-ring,
normal to have to gas blowby, normal to have blowby reaching
the secondary O-ring, and finally to the judgment that it was
normal to have erosion on the secondary ring.[16] The words of
NASA's Larry Wear say it all: "Once you've accepted an anomaly or something less than perfect, you know, you've given up
your virginity. You can't go back. You're at the point that it's
very hard to draw the line. You know, next time they say it's the
same problem, it's just eroded 5 mils more. Once you accepted
it, where do you draw the line? Once you've done it, it's very
difficult to go back now and get very hard-nosed and say I'm
not going to accept that."[17]

People in HROs worry a lot about the temptation to normalize unexpected events. They are well aware of the danger of
making false positive errors (diagnosing trouble where there is
none). But they have less fear of a false alarm than they have of
missing something significant that could escalate. For example,
a deckhand who loses a tool and reports the loss to a superior
may force the tower to shut down all launches and recoveries
of aircraft until the tool is found. But this person tends to be
praised rather than reprimanded, even if the report was a false
alarm, because something was done about a potentially unsafe
condition.

Feelings of Surprise

The moral in all this is the forewarning that perceptions of the unexpected are fleeting. You'll probably know when something unexpected happens. You'll know it because you'll feel surprised, puzzled, agitated, anxious, unsettled, frustrated, or even startled. Aviators call these feelings *leemers* (probably from *leery*); the feeling that something is not quite right, but you can't put your finger on it. Trust those feelings. They are a solid clue that your model of the world is in error. More important, try to hold onto those feelings and resist the temptation to gloss over what has just happened and treat it as normal. In that brief interval between surprise and successful normalizing lies one of your few opportunities to discover what you don't know. This is one of those rare moments when you can significantly improve your understanding. If you wait too long, normalizing will take over and you'll be convinced that there is nothing to learn. Most opportunities for learning come in the form of brief moments. And one of the best moments for learning, a moment of the unexpected, is also one of the most short-lived moments. People in HROs try to freeze and stretch out their unexpected moments in order to learn more from them. This is what happens during their lengthy after-action reviews.

■ The Idea of Mindfulness

By now it should be clear that it pays to be aware of your expectations. Expectations act like an invisible hand that guides you toward soothing perceptions that confirm your hunches, and away from more troublesome ones that don't. But it is these very same troublesome perceptions that foreshadow surprises, the unexpected, and tougher problems. If you depend too much on a simple set of expectations, unusual events can develop to more serious levels before you even notice them. People in HROs try to weaken the grip of this invisible hand of expectations so they can see more, make better sense of what they see, and remain more attuned to their current situation. They do this by means of at least the five processes mentioned briefly at the end of Chapter One: preoccupation with mistakes, reluctance to simplify, sensitivity to operations, commitment to resilience, deference to authority. These processes encourage people to be self-conscious about the validity of their beliefs and to question them, reaffirm them, update them, replace them, and learn from all these activities. These diverse activities hang together because they produce what we have called a state of *mindfulness*.

Mindfulness Defined

By *mindfulness* we mean the combination of ongoing scrutiny of existing expectations, continuous refinement and differentiation of expectations based on newer experiences, willingness and capability to invent new expectations that make sense of unprecedented events, a more nuanced appreciation of context and ways to deal with it, and identification of new dimensions of context that improve foresight and current functioning.[18] That is a mouthful. But sometimes it takes a large and complex idea to capture a large and complex phenomenon. As shown throughout this book, it is the very willingness and ability of HROs to organize in a complex manner that helps them deal with a complex world of the unexpected. Likewise, we need a complex set of ideas to understand just what they are doing and why it works. If you build similar complexity into your own managerial style, you, too, can do a better job of managing the complexities of the unexpected.

Mindfulness Contrasted with Mindlessness

To get a better idea of what mindfulness is all about, think about its opposite, the state of mindlessness. Mindlessness is what we saw when the Union Pacific tried to absorb the Southern Pacific

Railroad. In that example people found it hard to stay on top of things. Early warning signs of danger went unnoticed. Changes in context went unnoticed. Outdated diagnoses of problems went unnoticed. There was an underlying style of mental functioning in which people tried to implement the merger by following recipes, imposing old categories to classify what they saw, acting with some rigidity, operating on automatic pilot, and mislabeling unfamiliar new contexts as familiar old ones.

All these tendencies are examples of mindlessness. When people function mindlessly they don't understand either themselves or their environments, but they feel as though they do. They feel that because they have routines to deal with problems, this proves that they understand what's up. Although there is a grain of truth to that inference, what they fail to see is that their routines are little more than expectations that are subject to the very same traps as any other expectation. Whenever a routine is activated, people assume that the world today is pretty much like the world that existed at the time the routine was first learned. As with most expectations, people tend to look for confirmation that their existing routines are correct. And over time, they come to see more and more confirmation based on fewer and fewer data. What is missing are continuing efforts to update the routines and the perceptions, expectations, and actions that accompany them.

A silent contributor to mindlessness is the zeal found in most firms for planning. What people forget is that plans act the same way as expectations. They guide people to search narrowly for confirmation that the plan is correct. Disconfirming evidence is avoided, and plans lure you into overlooking a buildup of the unexpected quite as handily as do other expectations. This is not entirely surprising, since you may also recall that when we described expectations, much of the imagery we used was similar to the imagery people use when they talk about plans. We said that expectations could be understood as assumptions that *guide* choices, as suggestions of how the world *will react* to your actions, and as *hypotheses* waiting to be tested. If you understand the problems that expectations create, you understand the problems that plans create. And you may begin to understand why a preoccupation with plans and planning makes it that much harder for you to act mindfully.

By contrast, mindfulness is essentially a preoccupation with updating. It is grounded in an understanding that knowledge and ignorance grow together.[19] When one increases so does the other. Mindful people accept the reality of ignorance and work hard to smoke it out, knowing full well that each new answer uncovers a host of new questions. The power of a mindful orientation is that it redirects attention from the expected to the irrelevant, from the confirming to the disconfirming, from the pleasant to the unpleasant, from the more certain to the less certain, from the explicit to the implicit, from the factual to the probable, and from the consensual to the contested. Mindfulness and updating counteract many of the blind spots that occur when people rely too heavily on expectations. It is these very same blind spots that conceal the early stages of eventual disruptions. And it is the removal of these blind spots that is an important part of managing the unexpected. People on carriers work hard to minimize blind spots. So do people in all HROs. By following their lead, you, too, can see more, head off trouble sooner, and build a track record where you too can have fewer than your fair share of accidents.

The Capability for Mindfulness

Whenever people update their understanding of what is happening, they essentially rework the ways they label and categorize what they see. They do at least three things: reexamine discarded information, monitor how categories affect expectations, and remove dated distinctions.

To rework one's categories mindfully means first to see just how much information is discarded when a specific event is treated as an instance of a class of events with similar characteristics. For example, if I'm the deck handler on a carrier, responsible for spotting aircraft so that the deck never gets gridlocked, I may categorize the people I work with into categories such as male-female, experts-novices, pilots-deckhands, younger-older, rural-urban, warm-cold, fast to react–slow to react, dumb-smart, or none or all of these. Categories help me gain control of my world, predict what will happen, and plan my own actions. Categories are crucial tools. Without them, I would have to reinvent every action I took because every single person and situation I face would be unique. Categories save me that trouble, and I welcome them because they conserve scarce mental resources of attention and thinking. But categories are also crude tools. They edit everything I see. I see an introvert's preference to be alone rather than with others, but I don't see that person's initiatives, ability to mentally simulate worst case scenarios, calmness under fire, or sense of humor. I do not see new things about that person if I remain fixated on the same old dimensions of my category.

Second, mindful reworking of categories also means that I pay close attention to their effect on my expectations. Expectations and categories are closely related. Each helps define the other. For example, if I label someone an expert, I expect that this person will have the answers and require less monitoring and be a good person to copy when I'm trying to figure out how to act. These expectations may pan out. They may not. If I label others as slow to react, I expect that I will have to cut them some slack and exaggerate or repeat my orders to them and assign them less crucial activities during high-tempo periods. To rework expectations like this, I try to see whether they help in my efforts to manage the unexpected. As a result of this reflection, I may differentiate those expectations, replace them, supplement them, consolidate them, or discard the whole category.

Third, mindful reworking means that I check whether my categories remain plausible, or whether they have become out-of-date and can be improved. Continued reliance on dated, implausible distinctions virtually ensures trouble, since I know less about what is happening than I think I do. Recall that this is the basic misreading that haunts HROs. Failure to grasp what is going on means that unanticipated consequences are inevitable. If, for example, I assume that new naval recruits have rich imaginations and can improvise, an assumption I've always made, but fail to recognize that in fact most recruits now have impoverished imaginations because of the dulling influence of television, my continuing reliance on recruits for resilience may suddenly produce all kinds of unexpected trouble. The trouble starts the moment I refuse to act mindfully toward my categories and expectations. The trouble starts when I fail to notice that I see only whatever confirms my categories and expectations but nothing else. The trouble deepens even further if I kid myself that seeing is believing. That's wrong. It's the other way around. Believing is seeing. You see what you expect to see. You see what you have the labels to see. You see what you have the skills to manage. Everything else is a blur. And in that "everything else" lies the developing unexpected event that can bite you and undermine your best intentions.

Mindfulness exploits the fact that two key points of leverage in managing the unexpected are expectations and categories. People who persistently rework their categories and refine them, differentiate them, update them, and replace them notice more and catch unexpected events earlier in their development. That is the essence of mindfulness.

■ Mindfulness on Aircraft Carriers

Mindfulness is not some kind of unattainable ideal. HROs are living testimony that mindfulness can be attained and that it need not reduce production. Take the case of carriers. Their flight operations incorporate the same five processes of mindfulness that we find in other HROs. These are the same five processes that were in short supply at the Union Pacific.

First, people on carriers are *preoccupied with failure.* Every landing is graded and the grades are used to improve performance. Every landing is also televised throughout the ship so that everyone sees how everyone else performs. Near misses are debriefed within the hour and everyone is required to write down what they saw and heard prior to the incident. Small failures such as a plane in the wrong position on a full deck or a pilot's continued inability to snag the third arresting wire when landing are treated as signs of potential, larger problems within the system such as poor communication among deck handlers or inadequate training protocols for the Air Wing.

Second, people on carriers are *reluctant to simplify.* They take nothing for granted. They do not assume that any aircraft is ready for launch until it has been checked in multiple ways by redundant inspections. Hand signals, voice signals, and colored uniforms are used to convey information about who is responsible for what. If a pilot whose plane is positioned on a catapult for launch is then told to reduce engine power, he won't do so for fear of being launched at reduced power into the ocean. He keeps full power on until the catapult officer walks directly in front of his plane and stands directly over the two million horsepower catapult and signals that he should reduce power. Of course the catapult officer will not do that until he visually confirms that the catapult is safe and can't be fired.

Third, people on carriers maintain continuous *sensitivity to operations.* Officers from the captain on down are in continuous communication during flight operations and exchange information about the status of the activity. The entire ship is attuned to launching and recovering aircraft. The captain, who is in charge of the carrier, and the commander of the Air Wing, who is in charge of the aircraft, are positioned physically to observe all steps of the operations. Insensitivity to operations was clearly evident in a near miss that could have been catastrophic. The carrier was running at high speed in heavy seas when a request was made that it slow down so that aircraft could be moved from the flight deck down to the hangar deck on the deck edge elevator. The ship had other priorities and did not slow down immediately. Growing impatient and thinking the seas had calmed down, the deck officer ordered the elevator lowered. Seven men and an aircraft were washed overboard. All were rescued, itself an amazing feat.

Fourth, people on carriers have a *commitment to resilience.* Crews know the importance of routines and predictable behavior, as well as doing what they are told. They also know that no one understands the technology, the situation, or the people completely, so surprises are inevitable. And with surprise comes the necessity to improvise, make do with the hand you are dealt, adapt, think on your feet, and contain and bounce back from unexpected events. For example, when Dick Martin, the first captain of the carrier *Carl Vinson,* found himself in an intense storm off the coast of Virginia in 1983, the winds were so strong that he drove the carrier at ten knots in *reverse* in order to reduce the speed of the winds across the deck and allow the aircraft to land more safely. Rochlin[20] describes a maximum strike launch in which the first aircraft to be put on the catapult malfunctioned and could not be cleared from the catapult. The entire launch had to be reconfigured, and this necessitated the launch of an additional refueling tanker, new strategies for the raid, and new emergency fields. The reconfiguration was finished in less than ten minutes. Resilience like this is possible because people on carriers have deep knowledge of technologies, people, and capabilities.

And fifth, people on carriers maintain *deference to expertise.* The boss of an air squadron who knows the quirks of his own pilots may momentarily override higher-ranking officers in the tower and decide how planes will be landed when a member of his squadron loses hydraulics while attempting to land.

Despite their success in avoiding costly mistakes, no one on a carrier understands carrier operations perfectly or with complete certainty. But the same holds true for any HRO. And it certainly holds true for any organization you've ever been part of. What this means is that it is impossible to manage any organization solely by means of mindless control systems that depend on rules, plans, routines, stable categories, and fixed criteria for correct performance. No one knows enough to design such a system so that it can cope with a dynamic environment. Instead, designers who want to hold dynamic systems together have to organize in ways that evoke mindful work. People have to find it easy and natural and rewarding to adopt a style of mental functioning whereby they include, as part of their job description, the responsibility to engage in continuous learning as well as in the ongoing refinement and updating of emergent expectations. Carriers are guided as much by enlightened, updated expectations as they are by computation and analytic targets. If you want to manage the unexpected more skillfully, you would do well to follow the lead of carriers, where significant effort is invested in mindfulness, and significant penalties are assessed for mindlessness.

CHAPTER SUMMARY

Small moments of inattention and misperception can escalate into serious adverse events. A recurring source of misperception lies in the temptation to normalize an unexpected event in order to preserve the original expectation. The tendency to normalize is part of a larger tendency to seek confirmation for our expectations and avoid disconfirmation. This pattern ignores vast amounts of data, many of which suggest that trouble is incubating and escalating.

To counteract the temptation to seek confirmation and avoid disconfirmation, people on aircraft carriers strive for mindful updating. Mindful updating is facilitated by processes that focus on failures, simplifications, operations, resiliencies, and expertise. Mindful updating works because it treats reliability as a dynamic nonevent and encourages the continuing mutual adjustments that enact safe, reliable performance. Mutual adjustment rests on an infrastructure of respectful interaction, attentiveness, communication, and competence. Most organizations take this infrastructure for granted and in doing so allow it to decay. As it decays, alertness declines and surprises get bigger and more disruptive and require much more substantial administrative interventions to correct. The moral is, the invisible hand of expectations can be made visible by mindful action. Once made visible, the guidance provided by expectations can be redirected in ways that facilitate coping with the unexpected. And better coping means fewer pressing problems.

A Closer Look at Process and Why Planning Can Make Things Worse

W e turn now to a closer look at the five processes that produce mindfulness and enable HROs to maintain reliable performance while dealing with the unexpected. In this chapter we want to present a detailed picture of how mindfulness is implemented, so that you can get leads for ways to improve this capability in your own firm and in your own managing. In the previous chapter we looked at one kind of HRO, the aircraft carrier, and used it to illustrate how effective performance in dynamic environments hinges on the expected, the unexpected, and mindfulness. Here we use a different kind of HRO, nuclear power plants, to illustrate organizational processes that create mindfulness.

Everyone accepts that nuclear power generation is a complex, hazardous technology. What is not widely appreciated is how daunting an administrative and organizational task it is to manage nuclear power plants safely.[1] Nuclear power plant operations require almost four times more employees than conventional fossil-fueled steam-generating plants to produce a similar amount of electricity and operate reliably. At the Diablo Canyon nuclear power plant in San Luis Obispo, California, for example, there are approximately 1,250 employees on site during standard operations. During scheduled maintenance overhauls or outages, this number increases dramatically with the addition of over 1,100 outside consultants, support staff, and service contract workers. In contrast, a conventional fossil-fueled steam-generating plant located near Pittsburg, California, has 287 employees on site, and typically needs no more than twenty-five additional employees under contract to do its largest overhaul job.[2]

In addition to the unusually large number of employees to be managed, there is an unusually high level of interdependence between the parts of the system. Paul Schulman points out that whereas an air traffic control network can be decomposed to raise safety, as when traffic is kept out of a sector, separations between planes are increased, or planes are denied clearance to land or take off, the technology of nuclear power does not readily allow itself to be decomposed or simplified for safety. These qualities make it hard to analyze and act on the unexpected problems that arise. And if serious unexpected problems do arise that require a shutdown for even a short time, a 1993 estimate suggests that it costs about $100,000 per hour.[3] This gives some indication of just what is involved for the Pacific Gas and Electric Corporation to manage the technology of nuclear power. The number of employees, the high degree of interdependencies, the complexity of nuclear technology, the current regulatory climate, and relentless public scrutiny all add pressure to manage unexpected events well. And these pressures leave no room for error.

The better nuclear power generation plants do an especially good job converting mindfulness into workable processes that maintain alertness and updating. We can see mindfulness at work as clearly here as we could in carriers. In the remainder of this chapter we discuss the five processes in two sections: In the first section attention to failure, simplification, and operation are treated as mindful *anticipation* of the unexpected. In the second section attention to resilience and expertise are treated as mindful *containment* of the unexpected. Each process is discussed first as it is practiced in nuclear power plants and then as it is practiced elsewhere.

■ Anticipating and Becoming Aware of the Unexpected

Our identification of the five processes that produce mindfulness derives from our own review of years of research on HROs. We looked for what contributed to the high effectiveness of these organizations under trying conditions. How are they able to sustain their reliability in the face of persistent high risks and fluctuating conditions? What operational or organizational strategies allow them to respond effectively to sudden changes and unexpected events? The answer that emerged is the state of collective mindfulness that we described in the first two chapters as growing out of five qualities shared by the best HROs. Here we take a close-up look at the first three of these processes.

Some experts argue that it is impossible to anticipate the unexpected both because there are almost an infinite number of weak signals in the environment and because the ability to pick up these weak signals is far beyond the existing technological capabilities of most organizations.[4] Yet organizations that persistently have less than their fair share of accidents seem to be better able to sense the unexpected than other organizations that have more. Members of these organizations don't necessarily see discontinuities immediately, but they seem to see them earlier— soon enough to act before problems become severe. This ability to become aware of unanticipated events seems to be enhanced by the first three of our five processes: preoccupation with failure, reluctance to simplify interpretations, and sensitivity to operations.

Preoccupation with Failure

Mindfulness, in nuclear power plants and elsewhere, is partially the result of a preoccupation with failure. This process shows up over and over in HROs and is easily recognized in power generation. In fact, worries about failure are what gives nuclear power plants much of their distinctive quality. This distinctiveness arises from the simple fact that complete failures are a rare occurrence. So people in nuclear power plants are preoccupied with something they seldom see.

A preoccupation with failure is evident in frequent incident reviews, the reporting of errors no matter how inconsequential, and employees' obsession with the liabilities of success. MIT professor John Carroll has been especially alert to the role that incident reviews play in encouraging learning, self-analysis, knowledge sharing across boundaries inside and outside specific plants, and the development of problem resolution efforts.[5] It is natural to conduct a root cause analysis of major incidents such as damage to equipment or injuries to employees. But nuclear people pay just as much attention to minor incidents such as a fire door left open or work carried out without proper clearance. Such small incidents can combine and trigger a major problem.

A necessary component of an incident review is the reporting of an incident. And research shows that people need to feel safe to report incidents or they will ignore them or cover them up. Managerial practices such as encouraging questioning and rewarding people who report errors or mistakes strengthen an organizationwide culture that values reporting. Reporting is also encouraged because all employees recognize that complex nuclear technology can fail in ways that no one has imagined and that the technology is still capable of surprise.

But a preoccupation with failure is not unique to nuclear power plants. It is found in all kinds of organizations that have above-average success in managing the unexpected. For example, in the late 1990s Levi Strauss, the maker of iconic blue jeans first sold to the gold prospectors in the 1850s, discovered the importance of dwelling on failure because they had done just the opposite. They paid attention to success and grew complacent. "There's nothing as blinding as success," said Robert D. Haas, the beleaguered chairman of Levi Strauss & Company, to explain falling sales and an unexpected loss of their appeal to the young.[6]

What Haas discovered was something HROs discovered early on, namely, success has liabilities. New York University Business School professors Bill Starbuck and Frances Milliken spotted several of these liabilities when they reanalyzed the January 28, 1986, *Challenger* disaster that killed seven astronauts. "Success breeds confidence and fantasy. When an organization succeeds, its managers usually attribute success to themselves or at least to their organization, rather than to luck. The organization's members grow more confident of their own abilities, of their manager's skills, and of their organization's existing programs and procedures. They trust the procedures to keep them appraised of developing problems, in the belief that these procedures focus on the most important events and ignore the least significant ones."[7]

In effect, success narrows perceptions, changes attitudes, feeds confidence in a single way of doing business, breeds overconfidence in the efficacy of current abilities and practices, and makes leaders and others intolerant of opposing points of view.

The problem is that if people assume that success demonstrates competence, they are more likely to drift into complacency, inattention, and predictable routines. What they don't realize is that complacency increases the likelihood that unexpected events will go undetected and accumulate into bigger problems.

Members of HROs know there are limits to foresight. They know that they don't know, and they expect to be surprised. They know that all potential failure modes have not been experienced or exhaustively deduced. That is why people in HROs have been described as skeptical, wary, suspicious of quiet periods. But because failures are a rare occurrence in HROs, people in them are preoccupied with something they seldom see. And this poses something of a dilemma because it is through failure—often trial and error—that much learning in organizations occurs. But because the cost of failure is so high, and because the occurrence of failure so rare, HROs have fewer opportunities for learning. Therefore, they must find ways to do more with less information if they are to maximize what they can learn from the failures that do occur.

Effective HROs both encourage the reporting of errors and make the most of any failures that are reported. In fact, they tend to view any failure, no matter how small, as a window on the system as a whole. They view any lapse as a signal of possible weakness in other portions of the system. This is a very different approach from most organizations, which tend to localize failures and view them as specific, independent problems. We noted earlier that many nuclear power plants attend to small incidents in the belief that the accumulation of such incidents increases the probability of a major problem.[8] Members of power plants act as though there is no such thing as a confined failure and suspect, instead, that the causal chains that produced the failure are long and wind deep inside the system.

These behaviors are encouraged through leadership and management practices as well as an appropriate organizational design. Leaders put a premium on recruiting and selection processes and on developing an organizational capacity to train its members continuously in the physical and dynamic properties of the technical system. Effective decision making in nuclear power requires an understanding of the complexity of the work environment and the fact that it is an integrated system of interdependent parts. So individuals are trained to analyze both the upstream and the downstream consequences of their actions. Solutions that are too narrowly focused or too localized can lead to even worse consequences. The closure of one valve, for example, may increase pressure on others. Managers cultivate an atmosphere of open communication and teamwork and encourage individuals to actively monitor and challenge each other's actions and thought processes. Rewards and discipline in nuclear power plants are linked to these desired behaviors.

It is not simply a preoccupation with failures that enables successful HROs to keep their edge. People in HROs are preoccupied swiftly. They know that moments of learning are short-lived. And they convene people to uncover lessons learned faster than almost any other form of organization. The half-life of responsibility for errors is remarkably short. HROs respect that reality. Most other organizations don't. HROs learn from their mistakes as a result of swift processing. Most other organizations don't. For example, higher-performing nuclear power plants conduct almost daily interdepartmental incident reviews of seemingly minor slips that have no obvious link with consequential damage.[9] Behind this constant self-analysis is the idea that the technology can surprise them and that every problem, as minor as it is, reveals something about the health of the system as a whole. It also reflects the recognition that when people fail, they tend to be candid about what happened for a short period of time, and then they get their stories straight in ways that justify their actions and protect their reputations. And when official stories get straightened out and get repeated, learning stops. This mechanism is described in a colorful manner by historians who have studied mistakes in the military: "In the chaos of the battlefield there is the tendency of all ranks to combine and recast the story of their achievements into a shape which shall satisfy the susceptibilities of national and regimental vainglory . . . . on the actual day of battle naked truths may be picked up for the asking. But by the following morning they have already begun to get into their uniforms."[10]

The best HROs increase their knowledge base by encouraging and rewarding error reporting, even going so far as to reward those who have committed them. For example, industrial sociologist Ron Westrum describes the lesson conveyed when Wernher Von Braun sent a bottle of champagne to an engineer who, when a Redstone missile went out of control, reported that he may have caused a short-circuit during a prelaunch testing.[11] Analysis revealed that this indeed had caused the accident, and his confession meant that expensive redesigns were unnecessary.

Such an admission would have received a very different response in most organizations, just as it did when Ron Burns, the president of Union Pacific, admitted that UP had failed its shippers. Researchers Martin Landau and Donald Chisholm provide a similar example.[12] A seaman on the nuclear carrier *Carl Vinson* reported the loss of a tool on the deck. All aircraft aloft were redirected to land bases until the tool was found, and the seaman was commended for his action—recognizing a potential danger—the next day at a formal ceremony. Finally, Harvard Business School professor Amy Edmondson found, contrary to her hypotheses, that the highest-performing nursing units had higher detected rates for adverse drug events than did lower-performing units.[13] She interprets these results to mean not that more errors were committed in the high-performing units, but that a climate of openness made people more willing to report and discuss errors, work toward correcting them, and learn more about the system in the process.

One final characteristic that sets effective HROs apart from other organizations is how they perceive failure in relation to success. The most effective HROs regard close calls—for example, a near collision in aviation—as a kind of failure that reveals potential danger. In contrast, less effective HROs do just the opposite: They look at a near miss and see it as evidence of success and their ability to avoid disaster. When people see a near miss as success, this reinforces their beliefs that current operations are adequate to contain disasters. The example of the *Challenger* disaster presented in Chapter Two can be interpreted as precisely this kind of situation and is worth repeating. NASA repeatedly interpreted grease and burn marks behind the O-rings as within the limits of acceptable risk and therefore as a sign of the system's ability to avoid disaster. The problem was that the limits of acceptable risk kept changing. As people began to treat these warning signals as normal, they began to accumulate unnoticed. This was unfortunate, since these signals had a clear direction that indicated they were not randomly distributed.

Reluctance to Simplify Interpretations

A strong message of Chapter Two was that expectations simplify the world and steer observers away from disconfirming evidence that foreshadows unexpected problems. And mindfulness, with its insistence on closer attention to context, categories, and expectations was proposed as a way to counteract these simplifications. With closer attention to context comes more differentiation of worldviews and mindsets. And with more differentiation comes a richer and more varied picture of potential consequences, which in turn suggests a richer and more varied set of precautions and early warning signs. HROs are just as preoccupied with complicating their simplifications as they are with probing their failures. But just as it's hard to dwell on your failures rather than your successes, it's hard to refine your categories rather than lump them into actionable simplicities such as make or buy, friend or enemy, profit or loss. The difficulties notwithstanding, people in HROs are exemplary for their relentless attack on simplifications.

Two examples from nuclear power generation illustrate the resistance to simplification. A simple example: People who work in the power plant don't trust the simplifications found in drawings and blueprints.[14] If they have an assignment to shut down something such as the air supply in a nonoperating unit, they won't do so until they actually walk down the whole system, looking for valves, added piping, or reroutes that have been made since the drawings were completed. Those recent add-ons that are missing from the drawings are potential sources of serious surprises.

A more complex example: People who work with nuclear power use many of the same means to resist simplification that we saw in flight operations on aircraft carriers. The best example of this similarity is the reliance on constant interaction. Commenting on activity at Diablo Canyon, researcher Paul Schulman noted: "When faced with failure, members of the plant's departments can be readily observed in meetings, where they question the interpretation of other departments and add their own perspective on what's at risk in a proposed course of action. In effect, interacting with one another, employees generate hypotheses about what is going on, what can be done, and what the long-term, system-wide consequences of proposed actions might be. This is their way of coping with the potential for surprise within the enormously complex technology they are trying to control."[15]

It is not just interaction by itself that decreases simplification and increases mindfulness. It is the fact that the interaction is among people who have diverse expectations. This diversity enables people to see different things when they view the "same" event. We see this dynamic operating in many different places.

Almost all the oversight groups at Diablo Canyon (for example, equipment modification subgroup, regulatory nonconformance subgroup, incident investigation subgroup) have members from multiple units.[16] Since each unit has a different set of vested interests and a different set of expectations, its representatives see different things. When the oversight groups convene, they collectively see more and simplify less. The same holds true for the five people who work in the control room. They have quite different roles and expectations and see quite different things.

The following example taken from some earlier research illustrates our point about roles. "The lead person on the team is the shift foreman whose responsibility is to maintain the 'big picture' and not to get into details. There is a shift technical advisor who has engineering expertise and a senior control room operator who is the most senior person in the control room. Under the senior operator are the control room operator and the assistant control room operator, the latter being the person who has the newest operating license and who most recently has worked outside the control room."[17] Collectively, there is little that goes unnoticed in that control room, *if* the interaction is respectful.

That's a big *if* in nuclear power generation. Professor Paul Schulman states this point beautifully:

> Credibility and trust are perishable properties within any organization. They have to be continually nurtured and renewed if they are to survive. As the Diablo Canyon Operations Manager puts it, "Trust is important. You have to talk to people a lot to hold it." The Chemistry Department manager agreed: "Every day is a new day in interrelationships and in holding on to trust. It never gets institutionalized." . . . Credibility can vanish with departmental error, misunderstanding, or miscommunication. A constant stream of meetings seems to nurture credibility and trust. . . . It is perhaps no surprise that qualities frequently mentioned as highly valuable for plant personnel are friendliness

and skill in interpersonal relations. These qualities facilitate the development of credibility and trust needed among departments to effect the coordination of complex tasks. They are important elements in preventing jurisdictional antagonisms that could threaten operations at the plant.[18]

Simplifications produce blind spots, and HROs other than power plants also make substantial efforts to elaborate their simplifications. In doing so, they increase their capability for mindful management of the unexpected just as nuclear power plants do. A good way to spot these efforts is to apply this recipe: *It takes variety to control variety.* If people work in a varied, complex environment, those people need varied complex sensors to register the environmental complexities. Simple expectations produce simple sensing, which misses most of what is there. Simple sensors overlook both hints of the unexpected and a wider range of options to deal with it. A commander of an air group who has flown all the varieties of aircraft he controls is better able to sense what's up when an aircraft malfunctions unexpectedly, compared with someone who has flown fewer varieties of aircraft and is a less complex sensor. A loan officer who has made good and bad loans is a more complex sensor, able to sense more variety in his environment of clients, than is an officer who has made only good loans. A top management team whose members represent different functional backgrounds is a better sensing mechanism than is a team composed wholly of finance people, legal people, or engineers.

Sensitivity to Operations

People who run incident command systems at disasters such as air crashes and explosions have begun to adopt a three-layer command and control system that was worked out in Britain.[19] Three levels of management are specified: bronze command, which is operational; silver command, which is tactical; and gold command, which is strategic. Bronze involves routine tasks done by frontline teams at the scene (for example, putting water on a fire, ventilating a roof). Silver involves establishing priorities for allocating resources and coordinating actions (for instance, deployment of fire equipment as it arrives), a position that is often dependent on bronze commanders for first-hand observations and judgments. And gold command involves formulating overall policy for incident response and ensuring that tactical priorities are enforced, often off-site away from events (for example, a decision is made to suppress or contain the fire). The purpose of this design, frankly, is to keep the incident commanders from meddling too much in operations.[20] Commanders want to fight fire. They don't want to issue directives and then wait for cryptic feedback to tell them what is happening.

HROs have their own equivalent of a bronze, silver, gold hierarchy, but they run it differently. In HROs, for example, authority moves toward expertise, wherever it lies, and not up or down the hierarchy toward seniority or rank. We will discuss this adaptation when we get to the fifth process of mindfulness, *deference to expertise.* HROs work to reduce the differences among bronze, silver, and gold. And they also try to reverse the symbolic value of the colors. Bronze, the mundane level of operations, is actually treated as though it were the gold level that defines and drives the rest of the system. Prestige does not flow toward the big-picture planners. Quite the opposite. Operations are king. The key to effective performance lies in maintaining situational awareness, the big picture of current operations, or, in the language of aircraft carriers, having the bubble. In each case, people integrate information about operations and performance into a single picture of the overall situation and its operational status. When operations are treated as gold, this means that small interruptions in operations get undivided, widespread attention. And that, in turn, means that most beginnings of the unexpected get noticed and seldom grow larger. Lavishing this much attention on operations may seem like overkill and inefficient to boot. But when the stakes are high, when the system is operating close to the edge, and when redundancies designed into the system may make it more vulnerable rather than less so,[21] fuller attention to operations makes a lot of sense.

HROs are also run differently in the sense that they do not let hierarchies become dysfunctional bureaucracies,[22] they provide everyone with detailed real time information on what is happening,[23] and they instruct everyone to be on-call to do whatever the ongoing operations require. The big picture tends to be maintained more widely in HROs, with more people having the bubble.

All three of these customizations are visible in nuclear power plants. The plant manager at Diablo Canyon described control room operators as people who "have a bubble, a 3-D picture. They look at the control room and see the plant. If a needle goes up it should then come down. If not something's wrong. They have a mental picture in which once you learn the board you stop seeing it. You operate the plant as though it was an animal. The best operator is the guy who worked at the plant before it went on line. He crawled through the plant."[24] During outages at Diablo Canyon, meetings for outage updates and briefings are held throughout the day. These interdisciplinary and interdepartmental meetings are important for two reasons. First, they help nurture credibility and trust needed among departments to coordinate complex tasks. Meetings help prevent turf wars that could threaten operations at the plant. Second, constant interaction deepens people's understanding of the interdependent workings of the complex system itself. This helps people cope more effectively with unexpected surprises.[25] Professor Mathilde Bourrier found dense interaction in the handling of planned outages in the best nuclear power plants.[26] Top management people were available throughout the outage, so any problem could receive attention rapidly from all levels of the organization. This structure works largely because everyone also remains informed of what is happening and how the intervention is progressing.

The benefits of being sensitive to operations also show up in other contexts. For example, aircraft carriers accomplish this sensitivity through twenty real-time communication devices between the ship's control tower and people in the rest of the departments.[27] This results in both a dense web of communication and a dense picture of the situation. An example from the highly competitive and dynamic microcomputer industry reveals also that the best performers pay close attention to current operations. Decision makers in the higher-performing firms pay constant attention to real-time information.[28] They do this through frequent operations meetings, widely disseminated operational measures of performance, and nearly continuous face-to-face interaction. This sensitivity to operations "permits early identification of problems so that action can be taken before the problems become too substantial."[29]

Acting with Anticipation: A Summary

Reliability-enhancing organizations enact a number of processes to improve their capabilities to anticipate and become aware of the unexpected earlier, so people can act before problems become severe. We saw in our discussion that reliability-enhancing organizations

- Persuade all their members to be chronically worried about the unexpected and sensitive to the fact that in the face of the potential for surprise, any decision or action may be subject to faulty assumptions or errors in analysis.

- Work to create a climate where people feel safe to question assumptions and to report problems or failures candidly.
- Conduct incident reviews of unexpected events, no matter how inconsequential. They conduct them frequently and soon after something unexpected occurs—before people have a chance to revise their stories to justify their actions and protect their images.
- Help people expand the number of undesired consequences they envision so they can expand the number of precautions they will take.
- Encourage organizational members to view close calls as a kind of failure that reveals potential danger, rather than as evidence of success and their ability to avoid disaster.
- Create a climate where people are wary of success, suspicious of quiet periods, concerned about stability, routinization, and lack of challenge and variety that can predispose their organization to relax vigilance and sink into complacency that can lead to carelessness and error.
- Counteract tendencies to simplify assumptions, expectations, and analyses through practices such as adversarial reviews, selection of employees with nontypical prior experience, frequent job rotation, and retraining.
- Work to create a climate that encourages variety in people's analyses about the organization's technology and production processes, establish practices that allow those perspectives to be heard and to surface information not held in common. They also train people to manage these differences.
- Pay serious attention to operations, the front line, and imperfections in these features. They set in place operating practices that help people develop a collective cognitive map of operations at any one moment, such as situation assessments with continual updates and collective story building about actual operations and workplace characteristics.

■ Containing the Unexpected

No system is perfect. Sometimes precautions fail and unexpected events begin to escalate into a crisis. Then what? HROs of all kinds seem to have at least two processes that enable them to contain and bounce back from problems mindfully. These two involve commitment to building resilience and deference to expertise.

Commitment to Resilience

Nowhere in this book will you find any mention of perfection, zero errors, flawless performance, or infallible humans. That's because "[h]uman fallibility is like gravity, weather, and terrain, just another foreseeable hazard."[30] Error is pervasive. The unexpected is pervasive. By now that message should be clear. What is not pervasive are well-developed skills to detect and contain these errors at their early stages.

There is a good reason why such skills are in short supply. Managers are exhorted over and over to improve the old managerial standbys of anticipation and planning and vision and strategy. Neglected in all of the talk about foresight are the processes of resilience, intelligent reaction, and improvisation. That's a serious oversight. If errors are inevitable, managers should be just as concerned with cure as they now are with prevention. To be resilient is to be mindful about errors *that have already occurred* and to correct them before they worsen and cause more serious harm. If you take a close look at the phrase *managing the unexpected,* you will notice that the word *unexpected* refers to something that has already happened. When you manage the unexpected, you're always playing catch-up. You face something that you did not anticipate, but something that has happened anyway. And to cope with it requires a different

mindset than to anticipate its occurrence. This difference sometimes gets forgotten in even the best HROs. What also tends to
be forgotten is that we are not very good at foresight.[31]

Resilience plays a big role in nuclear power generation, but
not in the expected manner. People who work with nuclear
power are notorious for their obsession with anticipation. As of
May 1990, Diablo Canyon had 4,303 separate, multistep, written
procedures, each one revised up to twenty-seven times, that
were designed to anticipate and avoid problems with maintenance, operations, protection, and analysis. There are even procedures for drafting and altering procedures.[32] Researcher Paul
Schulman views this commitment to anticipation with approval,
noting that it removes uncertainty, promotes interdepartmental
coordination, provides a means to demonstrate technical virtu-
osity, sustains the belief that perfect operations are possible, provides a pretext for learning, protects individuals against blame,
discourages private informal modifications that are not disseminated, and provides a single focus for any changes and updates
in procedures. This is a compelling list of virtues.

But in the eyes of many, such a wholehearted commitment
to anticipation is also dangerous.[33] It presumes a level of understanding that is impossible to achieve when one is dealing with
unknowable, unpredictable, incomprehensible, complex technologies. It gives people the illusion that they have things under
control.[34] It blinds people to the very real possibility that each
new formalized procedure makes it that much harder to do the
work that is required.[35] Procedures begin to interfere with one
another, problems are concealed longer and incubate to more
advanced levels, and the discretion needed to fit the pieces together and make the system work is eliminated. A perfect example of how people lose flexibility in the face of extensive rules
and procedures is researcher Larry Hirschhorn's description of
the problems maintenance workers had when they needed to lift
wires to complete an assigned task in a nuclear plant but could

find no procedure for doing so.[36] Mechanics lifted the wire to complete their work. But this created a problem for the technicians assigned to test the motor before it was put back on-line because "the testing procedures did not cover the situation in which maintenance workers lifted the wires!"[37]

The point is that you cannot write procedures to anticipate all the situations and conditions that shape people's work. A commitment to anticipation has serious effects on what people expect and how they conduct themselves. Such a commitment assumes that uncertainty can be reduced and that the consequences of this reduction can be anticipated. Anticipation consumes great quantities of resources and attention. This happens because all solutions to all anticipated problems must be actively retained in the group's action repertoire and memory, so that any problem that arises can be matched with a predesigned solution. The mindset for anticipation is one that favors precise identification of possible difficulties so that specific remedies can be designed or recalled.

A commitment to resilience is quite different. The nature of a commitment to resilience is described by Wildavsky:[38] "The mode of resilience is based on the assumption that unexpected trouble is ubiquitous and unpredictable; and thus accurate advance information on how to get out of it is in short supply. To learn from error (as opposed to avoiding error altogether) and to implement that learning through fast negative feedback, which dampens oscillations, are at the forefront of operating resiliently." Resilient people think mitigation rather than anticipation. They are attentive to knowledge and resources that relieve, lighten, moderate, reduce, and decrease surprises. The mindset is one of cure rather than prevention. People are willing to begin treating an anomaly even before they have made a full diagnosis. They do so in the belief that their action will enable them to gain experience and a clearer picture of what they are treating. Unlike anticipation, which encourages people to think and then act, resilience encourages people to act while thinking or to act in order to think more clearly.

HROs overcome error when independent people with varied experience apply a richer set of resources to a disturbance at great speed and under the guidance of swift negative feedback. This is fast real-time learning that allows people to cope with an unfolding surprise in diverse ways that are unspecified in advance. In a curious inversion of common managerial images, managers in HROs take pride in the fact that they spend their time putting out fires, whereas most managers lament the time they devote to putting out fires. Managers in HROs regard successful firefighting as evidence that they are resilient and able to contain the unexpected. Most managers in business regard successful firefighting as evidence that they are distracted by daily nuisances and unable to do their "real work" of strategizing, planning, and anticipating.

HROs committed to resilience assume they will be surprised so they concentrate on developing general resources to cope and respond to change swiftly. This means they work to develop knowledge, capability for swift feedback, faster learning, speed and accuracy of communication, experiential variety, skill at recombination of existing response repertoires, and comfort with improvisation. At Diablo Canyon, for example, a commitment to resilience is evident in a culture that encourages the widespread conviction among all its members that formal procedures are fallible. The mindset is, Since we have not experienced all the ways in which things can fail, we must be continually wary.[39] A commitment to resilience is evident in training that is designed to (1) build people's skill in mentally simulating plant operations, how they can unravel, and how they might be corrected, and (2) develop their capabilities to cope with a disturbance and learn from their experience. A commitment to resilience is evident in management practices and organizational norms that encourage *conceptual slack*.[40] Conceptual slack refers to a divergence in organizational members' analytical perspectives about the organization's technology or production processes, a willingness to question what is happening rather than feign understanding, and greater usage of respectful interaction to accelerate and enrich the exchange of information.

Resilience is also found in other HROs. Researcher Gene Rochlin found that emerging crises on aircraft carriers are often contained by informal networks.[41] When events get outside normal operational boundaries, knowledgeable people self-organize into ad hoc networks to provide expert problem solving. These networks have no formal status and dissolve as soon as a crisis is over. Such networks allow for rapid pooling of expertise to handle events that are impossible to anticipate. The ability to come together informally as the situation demands increases the knowledge and actions that can be brought to bear on a problem. The result is that the organization has more skills and expertise to draw on. This flexible strategy for crisis intervention enables a system to deal with inevitable uncertainty and imperfect knowledge. This example also highlights the importance of generalized, uncommitted resources as a crucial component of resilience.

One of the best examples of resilience in a non-HRO setting comes from a more ordinary organization that experienced an unthinkable if not unanticipated event and handled it in a resilient manner. This organization is much closer to the kinds of organizations you are more familiar with.

On April 23, 1985, the Coca-Cola Company changed the taste of its premier product for the first time in ninety-nine years.[42] The reformulated product, called New Coke, was introduced at a splashy press conference at Lincoln Center in New York City. Within twenty-four hours, 81 percent of the U.S. population knew of the change, and early estimates suggested that 150 million people tried the new product. Despite careful planning and seemingly ample marketing research (almost $4 million was spent on research and taste tests), the situation quickly escalated into a disaster. Within the first four hours, the company received over 650 irate calls from customers who expressed negative reactions. Old Coke was stockpiled. There was talk by a group in Seattle of filing a class action lawsuit against Coca-Cola. Scalpers sold old Coke at premium prices. By mid-May, calls to the company averaged over five thousand per day and were accompanied by mountains of angry letters (40,000 by mid-summer). On July 11, top executives announced the decision to reintroduce the original formula under the trademark Coca-Cola Classic, thanked customers who were drinking New Coke, and reassured customers who wanted the original Coke that the company had heard their message.

The saga of New Coke highlights both the problems with anticipation and the benefits of resilience. A wholehearted commitment to anticipation, through planning and research, can be dangerous. It presumes a level of understanding that is impossible to achieve when one is dealing with uncertain and dynamic conditions. It gives people the illusion that they have things under control and it blinds them to the very real possibility that they may have gotten it wrong. During marketing trials, Coca-Cola researchers looked for evidence to confirm their decision to move ahead with the new formula and ignored evidence of unfavorable reactions. For example, most of the time the researchers tested whether people preferred a *sweeter* cola, not whether they favored the final formula that was chosen. Sweeter versions of anything tend to be preferred, but a preference for sweeter tasting products also tends to diminish over time. Moreover, researchers ignored the possibility that their assumptions were inaccurate. For example, when people were asked to pick their favorite cola in taste tests, they were not told that by picking one cola they would be *losing* the other one. None of these biases, however, is especially surprising if you consider that CEO Robert Goizueta had launched his era in 1981 by proclaiming that "change is imminent, nothing is sacred anymore, get used to that." The culture of Coca-Cola was permeated with the rhetoric of change. So, if you wanted to look good to top management, what better way was there than to stop treating the original Coke formula as sacred?

To the company's credit, they were able to react resiliently to events as they unfolded. They learned quickly through fast negative feedback. In just seventy-nine days they reversed course. They used the Fourth of July weekend as their deadline. If the sales of New Coke were unimpressive at that point, they vowed to take action. The sales of New Coke that weekend were unimpressive. So they improvised the brilliant response that allowed them to recover from a misstep that, at the time, was called the mistake of the century. Sales surged. Sales for 1985 were up 10 percent, profits were up 9 percent, the company had reaped an enormous amount of free publicity, and consumers came to see the company as fallible—just like them—and more responsive than most companies. And true to CEO Goizueta's pronouncement, nothing was sacred and everything had changed.

Deference to Expertise

To be mindful in the face of unexpected operating contingencies HROs have created a set of operating dynamics that are grounded in a deference to expertise. This process is *less* obvious than it looks. HROs don't simply assign the problem to an expert and then move on. Hierarchical patterns of authority certainly exist in HROs, as is typical of many large organizations. During routine operations, members of typical organizations demonstrate deference to the powerful, the coercive, the senior, and the experienced, forgetting that they may have had the same experience over and over, were never on the shop floor, are unfamiliar with the industry, were not around when the plant was constructed, or got their position through politics. Since people in these positions often get nothing but filtered good news, they continue to believe they are on top of things. Hierarchies and deference to power and politics are the rule. This can work against managing the unexpected. With every problem, someone somewhere sees it coming. But those people tend to be low rank, invisible, unauthorized, reluctant to speak up, and may not even know they know something that is consequential. Someone knew that Coca-Cola Company was looking at a disaster. Someone saw that Union Pacific trains were taking longer to complete their runs. Someone knew that ice on a launch pad was big trouble. But most people didn't know this and didn't want to know this. Those who did know weren't deferred to. What HROs have mastered is the ability to alter these typical patterns of deference as the tempo of operations changes and unexpected problems arise.

In a typical closed hierarchical structure, important choices are made by "important" high-ranking decision makers who can participate in many choices. In such structures, status and rank rather than expertise determines who makes the decisions. The decision structure in effective HROs, the structure that links decision makers with active choices, is a hybrid of hierarchy and specialization. The decision structure is hierarchical in the sense that important choices must be made by important decision makers, and important decision makers can participate in many choices. But the distinctive structural twist in HROs is that the designation of who is the "important" decision maker keeps changing based on the decision maker's specialty. The designation of who is important "migrates" to the person or team with expertise in that choice-problem combination. This migration achieves flexibility as well as orderliness. By blending a hierarchical decision structure with a specialist decision structure HROs recognize—and operationalize—a principle that often escapes decision makers at critical moments: Expertise and experience are usually more important than rank. HROs allow expertise at the bottom of the pyramid to rise to the top when needed. This increases the likelihood that new capabilities will be matched with new problems. But decisions migrate up as well. The direction of the migration depends on accountability, responsibility, uniqueness of the problem, and environmental characteristics.[43]

In HROs, decisions have to be made quickly and accurately, so problem sensors closest to the problem, often lower-level members, are empowered to make important decisions and are held highly accountable for these decisions. But accountability evokes uncomfortable feelings of high responsibility. This leads lower-level members to push decision making back up the hierarchy, especially when the event is unusually unique. Decisions also may be pushed up when political pressures or career concerns are high.[44]

Diablo Canyon is a good example. When its number two reactor tripped, "the plant manager stayed out of the control room and relied on 'root cause' analyses by his senior people who, in turn, relied upon their subordinates."[45] Bourrier describes a structure of this kind in outage planning at one of the nuclear power plants she studied.[46] She noted that there was neither a detailed plan nor a special structure to deal with the outage. Instead, the most important characteristic was "the formal delegation of power to craft personnel supported by a nearly complete availability of top management at all times. By being a very flexible and adaptive organization, any problem can rapidly receive the attention it requires at all levels of the organization." This mechanism allows the proficiency of the organization to come into play, provides checks and balances through oversight, and allows sequentially higher-level managers to take control of decisions should events begin to unravel.

Westrum[47] calls this pattern "coordinate leadership," which he describes as shifting the leadership role to the person who currently has the answer to the problem in hand. This depiction of how HROs enact flexibility is supported by field research of aircraft carriers and nuclear power plants. But it is not unique to these settings. We see references to it in studies of fast strategic decision making as well. Earlier we noted professor Kathleen Eisenhardt's conclusion that the highest performing firms in the dynamic microcomputer industry achieve their success, in part, because executives are sensitive to operations. Executives immerse themselves in real-time information on their firm's operations and environment. Eisenhardt also found that the most successful executives "use tactics to accelerate analysis of information and alternatives. . . . They also gather advice from everyone but focus their attention on the most experienced executive."[48] We also see this pattern in other dynamic high-stakes contexts—for example, in the better coronary care units. St. Elizabeth's Hospital in Ohio, ranked as one of the best coronary-care hospitals in the state,[49] encourages doctor-nurse interactions where nurses are free to "second-guess" even the chief of cardiac surgery when problems arise. At Loma Linda Children's Hospital the problem of accidental extubations of the endotracheal tube is handled as follows. When the nurse believes that the child's agitation may cause dislodgment of the tube, she or he asks the resident for an order to increase sedation. Residents have been taught to respect the nurse's recommendations. Requests by the nurse for an increase in medication are not denied.

This loosening of hierarchical constraints is facilitated by the mindful system in place in HROs. When people in effective HROs focus on failure, they treat every signal as though it were novel. This generates the attentiveness necessary to link expertise with problems, solutions, and decisions in the moment. This shift also reflects mindful action. When people examine an anomaly, they turn to others in an effort to understand what the anomaly means. This turn is a subtle loosening of hierarchy in favor of expertise. The "agency" that triggers this loosening is not an edict from the top, but rather a collective, cultural belief that the necessary capabilities lie somewhere in the system and that migrating problems will find them. This means decisions migrate down but they also migrate up. If people in HROs get into situations they don't understand, they're not scared to ask for help. In a macho world, asking for help, admitting that you're in over your head, is frowned upon. Good HROs don't allow that to happen. It is a sign of strength and confidence to know when you've reached the limits of your knowledge and know enough to enlist outside help.

Acting to Contain: A Summary

By definition, errors, surprises, and the unexpected are difficult to anticipate. Some organizations deal with this difficulty by trying to improve their ability to anticipate. They invest resources in activities such as building defenses in depth, developing elaborate contingency plans, imagining a greater range of worst case scenarios, avoiding obvious hazards, relying on "fire drills" to protect against expected surprise, and stabilizing the environment so that its variations are more predictable (for example, lobbying, alliances). The intention of all these efforts is to prevent bad outcomes before they occur. HROs do not ignore foresight and anticipation, but they are mindful of its limitations. Under the assumption that uncertainty is irreducible and that the sources of harm are limitless, HROs invest more of their resources to help people contain and bounce back from unexpected events after they begin to occur. We saw in our discussion that reliability-enhancing organizations

- Pay just as much attention to building capabilities to cope with errors that have occurred as they do to improving capabilities to plan and anticipate events before they occur.
- Develop capabilities for mindfulness, swift learning, flexible role structures, filling in for one another, quick size-ups, and elementary structuring of personnel (for example, adopt a bronze, silver, gold command structure).

- Adopt an organizationwide mindset of cure rather than pre-vention. This means people are attentive to knowledge and resources that relieve, lighten, moderate, reduce, and de-crease surprises. People are willing to begin treating an anomaly even before they have made a full diagnosis. They do so in the belief that this action will enable them to gain experience and a clearer picture of what they are treating. Unlike anticipation, which encourages people to think and then act, resilience encourages people to act while thinking or to act in order to think more clearly. A commander tries different tactics to learn what the enemy can do. This is em-pirical fighting. It is reactive. That is the intention.

- Encourage people to make knowledge about the system transparent and widely known. The more people know about the weaknesses of their system and how to manage them, the faster they can notice and correct problems in the making.

- Establish pockets of resilience through uncommitted re-sources such as informal networks of people who come to-gether on an as-needed basis to solve sticky problems.

- Create a set of operating dynamics that shifts leadership to the person who currently has the answer to the problem at hand. This means people put a premium on expertise over rank and decisions migrate both downward and upward as conditions warrant.

■ Conventional Mechanisms for Managing the Unexpected and Their Traps

Most organizations don't work the way we have just described. Traditional organizations typically try to defend against possi-ble threats through much more conventional mechanisms such as plans, standard operating procedures, professional rules, and informal prescriptions. These structural mechanisms can be effective because they reduce the amount of information that people have to process. This reduction supposedly enables people to manage everyday situations more effectively in order to achieve reliable outcomes. But a closer look suggests that these conventional mechanisms often compromise the capability for mindfulness, thereby actually intensifying threats.

Consider planning. Planning has been variously described as thinking about the future, designing a desired future and ways to bring it about, or consciously determining courses of action, as well as a formalized procedure to produce an articulated result in the form of an integrated system of decisions.[50] Organizations create plans to prepare for the inevitable, preempt the undesirable, and control the controllable. Rational as all this may sound, planning has its shortcomings. Because planners plan in stable, predictable contexts they are lulled into thinking that the world will unfold in a predetermined manner, a lapse that Mintzberg calls "the fallacy of predetermination."[51] When people are in thrall of predetermination, there is simply no place for unexpected events that fall outside the realm of planning.

Plans, in short, can do just the opposite of what is intended, creating mindlessness instead of mindful anticipation of the unexpected. They do so in at least three ways. First, since plans are built from assumptions and beliefs about the world, they embody expectations. As we saw earlier in the case of the Union Pacific, expectations have a downside. Strong expectations influence what people see, what they choose to take for granted, what they choose to ignore, and the length of time it takes to recognize small problems that are growing. Attention, interpretation, and action are colored by what people expect to see. Because there is so much ambiguous information in organizations, there is a need for structure of some kind. Expectations provide that structure. But when people impose their expectations on ambiguous stimuli, they typically fill in the gaps, read between the lines, and complete the picture as best they can. Typically this means that they complete the picture in ways that confirm what they expected to see. Slight deviations from the normal course of events are smoothed over and quickly lose their salience. It is only after a space shuttle explodes or illicit trading is exposed or vehicle tires come apart that people see a clear and ominous pattern in the weak signals they had previously dismissed.

By design, then, plans influence perception. In particular, plans reduce the number of things people notice. This occurs because people encode the world largely into the categories activated by the plan. Anything that is deemed "irrelevant" to the plan gets only cursory attention. And yet it is these irrelevancies, these data that exist outside the limits of our foresight, that are the seedbed of the unexpected events that make for unreliable functioning.

Second, plans can undercut organizational functioning because they specify contingent actions that are designed to cope with the future. The problem is, these contingent actions are doubly blind. They are blind because they restrict attention to what we expect. And they are blind because they limit our present view of our capabilities to those we now have. When we plan contingent actions, we tend not to imagine how we might recombine the actions in our current repertoire to deal with the unexpected. In other words, contingency plans preclude improvisation.

Third, plans presume that consistent high-quality outcomes will be produced time after time if people repeat patterns of activity that have worked in the past. The problem with this logic is that routines can't handle novel events. If unexpected events are to be managed, this means that people have to change what they do, but not their way of sensing that something needs to be done. And this is precisely the point that the most effective HROs seem to have grasped. They understand that reliable outcomes require the capability not only to sense the unexpected in a stable manner but also the capability to deal with the unexpected in a variable manner. HROs are able to implement this differentiated reaction because of their mindful infrastructure. For example, Schulman observed that operators at the Diablo Canyon nuclear power plant continually altered their actions and interactions to deal with the unexpected, but they did *not* alter their mindful processes of understanding, evidence collection, detection, evaluation, and revising.[52] These mindful processes became the stable routines that triggered the variable activities that managed the unexpected. Most organizations don't act this way. Under the influences of routines and expectations, they tend to keep their activities constant and vary their processes of mindfulness, precisely the opposite of what HROs do. When HROs act mindfully as a matter of routine, they are better able to notice early warnings that their comprehension of the world may be flawed. And with earlier warning, HROs are in a better position to create a response that controls problems before they enlarge and disrupt the entire system.

To manage the unexpected is to be reliably mindful, not reliably mindless. Obvious as that may sound, those who invest heavily in plans, standard operating procedures, protocols, recipes, and routines tend to invest more heavily in mindlessness than in mindfulness. A heavy investment in plans restricts sensing to expectations built into the plans and restricts responding to actions built into the existing repertoire. The result is a system that is less able to sense discrepancies, less able to update understanding and learn, and less able to recombine actions into new ways to handle the unexpected.

We interpret efforts by organizations to embrace the quality movement as the beginning of a broader interest in reliability and mindfulness. But some research shows that quality programs have led to only modest gains. As Richard Hackman and Ruth Wageman[53] argue, this might be the result of incomplete adoption.

But we would go even further, and argue that the reason for incomplete adoption is that the necessary infrastructure for reliable practice, as exemplified in HROs, is not in place even where TQM success stories are the rule. This conclusion is consistent with W. E. Deming's insistence that quality comes from broadbased organizational vigilance for problems other than those found through standard statistical process control methods.[54]

Our conclusion that crucial infrastructure is missing in quality programs is also consistent with suggestions that total quality management (TQM) efforts fail because organizations do not adjust their routine quality control practices to deal with more complex, emergent problems.[55] If one uses HROs as the standard for how to achieve reliability under trying conditions, it becomes clear that quality continues to be compromised because people still don't understand the mindsets, procedures, and patterns of wisdom to which HROs aspire. Aspirations for high reliability are rarely out of reach when people organize. What puts them out of reach are organizational designs that focus attention on efficiency, success, homogeneity, and certainty rather than on inefficiency, failure, diversity, and surprise. Mindful attention to balancing these competing objectives may be a signature of both the best HROs and the best qualityconscious organizations.

The point is that "good management" is less obvious than it seems. In dynamic environments, conventional practices of good management can conceal more than they reveal. Concealment occurs because good management tends to unfold at the mercy of expectations and at the mercy of all the blind spots that expectations create. When HROs practice good management, they do something different. They tend to act in ways that loosen the grip of expectations on their perception and interpretation. In doing so, they tend to see more. And they tend to see more, earlier, when they can do something about it.

CHAPTER SUMMARY

In this chapter we have elaborated on the five qualities of mindfulness and the organizational processes and leadership practices that contribute to a mindful infrastructure. These five qualities can be grouped under two broad headings: anticipating and becoming aware of the unexpected (preoccupation with failure, reluctance to simplify, and sensitivity to operations) and containing the unexpected when it does occur (commitment to resilience, deference to expertise). Systems that have these capabilities counteract traps that are built into expectations, detect the unexpected sooner, contain the unexpected more fully, and learn from these local and contingent responses.

We also looked more closely at how many of the conventional mechanisms used by non-HROs to cope with unexpected events actually make things worse. Plans, operating procedures, and the like have effects that run exactly counter to the processes of mindfulness. Plans, for example, embody expectations and thus narrow perceptions by reducing the range of things that people notice. The typical organization's emphasis on routine and contingency planning embodies assumptions that weaken the ability to respond to the unexpected and foster new learning. This is the antithesis to the processes of mindfulness essential to achieving reliable outcomes in an increasingly complex and volatile world. The reason these qualities are not more visible and influential is that most organizations look for lessons on how to survive from organizations like themselves. They should look instead to organizations that, on the surface, look quite different: high reliability organizations that have, of necessity, learned how to manage the unexpected.

Assessing Your Capabilities for Assured Performance

S o far we have discussed the ideas of the expected, the unexpected, and mindfulness and why the five processes that
create mindfulness are crucial to high performance in a
complex and uncertain world. In these final three chapters, we
turn to the question of how to implement the results of this
analysis. We begin by presenting an audit you can conduct to
see how mindful your own organization is.

Winston Churchill provides a good example of the kind of
self-conscious auditing we are concerned with in this chapter.
During World War II Churchill made the horrifying discovery
that Singapore was far less impregnable than he thought and was
actually highly vulnerable to a Japanese land invasion. Reflecting

on this unexpected discovery, Churchill commented in his history of the war, "I ought to have known. My advisors ought to have known and I ought to have been told, and I ought to have asked."[1] Churchill's audit consisted of four questions: Why didn't I know, why didn't my advisors know, why wasn't I told, why didn't I ask? Just imagine what would happen if, after a disruptive event occurred, people used Churchill's protocol to discuss it. Such a discussion would increase everyone's awareness of the nature of mindfulness, and it would go a long way toward alerting them to the early stages of an unexpected event.

Here is a situation similar to Churchill's. On March 6, 1987, the ferry boat *Herald of Free Enterprise* capsized and sank within five minutes when it left the dock at Zebrugge, Belgium, with its bow doors open. The tragedy resulted in the loss of 193 lives. As with any vessel, there were several standing orders. Order 01.09, Ready for Sea, reads "Heads of Departments are to report to the Master immediately if they are aware of any deficiency which is likely to cause their departments to be unready for sea in any respect at the due sailing time. In the absence of any such report the Master will assume, at the due sailing time, that the vessel is ready for sea in all respects."[2] What is interesting here is that this standing order violates two of Churchill's four requirements. It violates the requirement that his informants should have informed him, and it violates the requirement that he should have inquired of them. Philosopher Robert Allinson puts the point this way:

> Order 01.09 would seem to be worded in such a way as both not to require those in a position to know to make a report and not to require those to whom a report is being made to ask for the conclusions of a report. The total absence of a report is taken to be sufficient that the ship is ship shape. Thus, this order is two steps away from Churchill's requirements. It would not even meet his requirements if it were to state that

a report must be made. It would further require that there must be a request for such a report in the case that there was a failure to report.[3]

The problem with the standing order is obvious, but tricky. If you hear nothing, then you assume that things are safe. But another reason you may hear nothing is that things are *not* safe. The reporter may be incapacitated—a signal of great danger. This was the case with the *Herald of Free Enterprise.* The seaman who was responsible for closing the bow doors had fallen asleep in his cabin and did not awake until he was thrown out of his bunk as the boat capsized. Here we bump up against the issue of a default position: What does it mean when there is no news? Does it mean that things are going well, or that they are going poorly, or that it is unclear how things are going? An organization's "default" answer tells us something important about the degree to which the organization is mindful. And that in turn begins to tell us something about how well or how poorly it is likely to deal with the unexpected.

These are the kinds of questions that are the focus of this chapter. We will present several instruments designed to help you and your organization become more alert to the dimension of mindfulness and mindlessness as it permeates your work and your system. The purpose of the instruments is to help you be more attentive to moments when you or your organization are working on automatic pilot and those more mindful moments when you tend to treat preexisting labels, categories, and contexts as less well known, more dynamic, and more in need of updating than is presumed by your routines. This mindfulness audit is a first step toward helping your firm experience a greater number of mindful moments.

Before we tackle this job, there is a caution. Mindful moments are important if the contexts in which you operate are dynamic, ill structured, ambiguous, unpredictable. In less dynamic contexts, mindfulness is less necessary and the economies of mindlessness are more appropriate. Mindfulness takes effort and cost; mindlessness in the form of routine can be cost-efficient. The trouble is that this is not nearly as neat and tidy as it sounds. All of us like to have our expectations confirmed, which means we are likely to overestimate the degree to which what we face is well structured, clear, and predictable. Hence, we are mindless more often than we should be. That is why the unexpected so often makes such deep inroads before it is detected. Since the unexpected develops to an advanced stage before we notice it, it produces greater disruption.

The audit presented in this chapter should assist you in spotting more and less mindful behavior. It is also intended to help you develop more awareness of how to institutionalize mindfulness by spotting analogues of the five HRO processes in your own firm. Where are those analogues? How well developed are they? Do they produce similar outcomes of mindfulness that they produce in HROs?

In the following discussion we look separately at mindfulness and the five processes that produce it. We introduce each set of items by first reviewing the ideas and concepts that generated them. We do this so you can see why the items are worded the way they are, and which aspects of mindfulness are being assessed. More important, since you will know the general ideas that lie behind specific items, you can use those ideas to craft additional items that may be more sensitive to the idiosyncrasies of your firm. The goal of this exercise is to help you see how you stack up in comparison to best practices in HROs. If customizing some of the items helps you make that assessment, then feel free to do so.

We encourage you to take the audit and then ask others in your company to do the same. We have included scoring guidelines at the bottom of each instrument to help you interpret your current infrastructure and capabilities for mindfully managing the unexpected. Try to predict how people at different hierarchical levels, functions, specialties, and locations within your own organization might answer these questions. Later we will explain in more detail how to interpret and use the results. For now, answer the questions for yourself and imagine how members of your work unit, department, or executive team might answer them.

■ What Do You Count On? A General Starting Point

Here is the background for the set of items that you will find in Exhibit 4.1. When organizations are set apart and referred to as *reliability centered or reliability enhancing,* the intention is to highlight their ability to remain failure free under conditions that threaten both safety and production. The survival of high reliability organizations depends on reliable performance under conditions of constant surprise. These organizations are distinctive precisely because they let fewer unexpected events blow up into crises. People in HROs are just like people in other organizations in the sense that they don't know beforehand what will go wrong. Unlike people in most other organizations, however, they have a good sense of what needs to go right and a clearer understanding of the factors that might signal that things are unraveling. Because people in HROs are united in this awareness, everyone is alert to unanticipated possibilities. Hence, they become aware of unforeseen events more quickly and act more quickly to contain them. As a result, unexpected problems do not persist or combine with other problems. People act with flexibility earlier rather than later, when it is easier to correct deviations and when there are more possible courses of action. Later on, when the problem grows bigger, one's choice of solutions is constrained.

We have attributed this flexibility in managing the unexpected to five qualities that create a mindful infrastructure. A

Exhibit 4.1. A Starting Point for Your Firm's Mindfulness.

How well do each of the following statements characterize your organization? Enter next to each item below the number that corresponds with your conclusion: 1 = not at all, 2 = to some extent, 3 = a great deal.

1. There is an organizationwide sense of susceptibility to the unexpected.

2. Everyone feels accountable for reliability.

3. Leaders pay as much attention to managing unexpected events as they do to achieving formal organizational goals.

4. People at all levels of our organization value quality.

5. We spend time identifying how our activities could potentially harm our organization, employees, our customers, other interested parties, and the environment at large.

6. We pay attention to when and why our employees, our customers, or other interested parties might feel peeved or disenfranchised from our organization.

7. There is widespread agreement among the firm's members on what we don't want to go wrong.

8. There is widespread agreement among the firm's members about how things could go wrong.

Scoring: Add the numbers. If you score higher than sixteen, the *mindful infrastructure* in your firm is exemplary. If you score between ten and sixteen, your firm is on its way to building a mindful infrastructure. Scores lower than ten suggest that you should actively be considering how you can immediately improve your firm's capacity for mindfulness.

mindful infrastructure has to be directed toward something. And that something for HROs is a clear, broadly shared understanding of what it is that people want to go right, and how it might go wrong. The question of how well people understand these things in your organization is as good a place as any to start an audit of mindfulness.

A key concept behind the audit is the idea of reliability. To describe something as reliable is to describe "what one can count upon not to fail in doing what is expected."[4] Taking this definition literally suggests that to be a reliable organization is to be concerned with at least three questions:

- What do people count on?
- What do people expect from those things they count on?
- In what ways can those things people count on fail?

The answers to these three questions should provide important clues about what it is that could go wrong that you don't want to go wrong. To move toward a more mindful system and higher reliability is to enlarge what people monitor, expect, and fear. To move toward a less mindful system and lower reliability is to reduce those three.

The point about enlarging awareness is crucial. You may have noticed that there are several places in our argument where the word *focus* fits well, but we don't use it. We steer clear of that word for a reason that you should consider. *Focus* excludes; *enlarge* includes. Recall that people in HROs tend to be inclusive. They interpret untoward events, near misses, or failures as symptoms that give clues about the health of the system as a whole. High reliability organizations are distinguished by the breadth of what people monitor, expect, and fear. Less breadth should mean more occasions for surprise, and less reliability. Therefore, when you do an audit, listen for the word *focus*. It may signal a red flag. You can uncover important clues about what you expect and the ways your expectations can fail by probing ways in which unexpected events might negatively affect people or other entities who have an interest in your firm or on whom you are dependent. Answers to the questions in Exhibit 4.1 will provide insight into whether people are conscious of potential problems and how open they are to finding out. Mindfulness increases as people become more conscious about the ways in which the system can be disrupted, what might go wrong, and who these disruptions are likely to harm. And when mindfulness increases, people are less likely to deny that unexpected surprises can happen or to rationalize away the potential consequences.

■ Appraising Tendencies Toward Mindlessness

The idea of mindfulness originally meant a mental orientation in which there is ongoing active refinement and differentiation of categories, an ongoing willingness and capability to invent new categories that carve streaming events into more meaningful sequences, and a more nuanced appreciation of context and ways to deal with it.[5] In contrast, a tendency toward mindlessness is characterized by a style of mental functioning in which people follow recipes, impose old categories to classify what they see, act with some rigidity, operate on automatic pilot, and mislabel unfamiliar new contexts as familiar old ones. A mindless mental style works to conceal problems that are worsening.

An audit of mindlessness is more than a simple assessment of attention, preoccupation, or the factors that distract or interfere with people's attention. It is a deeper probe into how often people come into contact with the unexpected in their day-to-day activities, how strongly people expect that things will go as planned, and how strong their tendencies are either to solve or to ignore the disruptions that unexpected events produce. Instances of mindlessness occur when people confront weak stimuli, powerful expectations, and strong desires to see what they want to see. This is another way of saying that people and organizations are mindless when they face weak or confusing signals and rely on past categories, normalize the confusing signals, act on automatic pilot, and hold onto their perspective without awareness that things could be otherwise. Hence, a more systematic audit of tendencies toward mindlessness would assess the incidence of weak stimuli and strong expectations, when people are motivated to ignore unexpected surprises, and what resources managers and organizations use to overcome these conditions.

Mindlessness is more likely when people are distracted, hurried, or overloaded. To deal with production pressures, people ignore discrepant cues and cut corners. But mindlessness also occurs when people cannot do anything about what they see. The close relationship between mindfulness and the action repertoire in HROs is a key to their effectiveness. Industrial sociologist Ron Westrum claims that organizations that are willing to act on specific surprises are also organizations that are willing to see those surprises and think about them.[6] What this means is that when people bring new domains under their control and enlarge their ability to act on them, they also enlarge the range of issues they can notice in a mindful manner. For example, if people don't know how to learn from mistakes, they are not likely to notice many of their own mistakes, since they don't know what to do with them. If, however, they improve their capability to conduct thorough postmortems of what went wrong and to implement the lessons learned, they are likely to notice more mistakes because now they can do something about them. Conversely, if people are unable to act on surprises, it is not long before their "useless" observations of those surprises are also ignored or denied, with the result that events go unnoticed and can cumulate into bigger problems. Moreover, people with a limited action repertoire often impose old categories to classify what they see and mislabel unfamiliar new problems as familiar old ones so they can act on them. For example, if firms traditionally decouple authority from responsibility and hold frontline people responsible for outcomes, but don't give them the authority to ensure those outcomes, this limited way of working may well be imposed mindlessly on new fast-paced situations where high performance is possible only when responsibility and authority coincide. There's more than a grain of truth to the saying that when you have a hammer every problem looks like a nail.

When these various sources of mindlessness are combined, they form a picture of an organization that knows little about itself, may not realize that its knowledge is impoverished, and persists in doing traditional monitoring that produces few updates. This is the nonmindful world that is reflected by questions such as those presented in Exhibit 4.2. The questions provide a window into your vulnerability to mindlessness because they reveal how strong people's tendencies are to ignore the disruptions that unexpected events cause.

■ Rudiments of Mindfulness

Being prone to mindlessness is one way that organizations may fail in managing the unexpected. Another is being averse to mindfulness. The items in Exhibit 4.3 assess aversion to mindfulness. The rudiments of mindfulness are a willingness to doubt that one's current picture is complete, a willingness to inquire further to remove some of those doubts, and a desire to update situational awareness on a continuing basis. Most fully developed processes of mindfulness presume these three basics. Therefore, an early assessment of these precursors provides some idea of your group's readiness for a more substantial set

Exhibit 4.2. Assessing Your Firm's Vulnerability to Mindlessness.

How well do each of the following statements describe your work unit, department, or organization? Enter next to each item below the number that corresponds with your conclusion: 1 = not at all, 2 = to some extent, 3 = a great deal.

1. During a normal week, exceptions rarely arise in our work. _____

2. The situations, problems, or issues we encounter are similar from day to day. _____

3. People in this organization have trouble getting all the information they need to do their work. _____

4. People are expected to perform their jobs in a particular way without deviations. _____

5. People often work under severe production pressures (that is, time, costs, growth, or profits). _____

6. Pressures often lead people to cut corners. _____

7. There are incentives in the work environment to hide mistakes. _____

8. People have little discretion to take actions to resolve unexpected problems as they arise. _____

9. Many people lack the skills and expertise they need to act on the unexpected problems that arise. _____

10. People rarely speak up to test assumptions about issues under discussion. _____

11. If you make a mistake, it is often held against you. _____

12. It is difficult to ask others for help. _____

Scoring: Add the numbers. If you score higher than twenty-four, the current potential for *mindlessness* is high and you should be actively considering how you can immediately improve the capability for mindfulness. If you score between fourteen and twenty-four, the potential for *mindlessness* is moderate. Scores lower than fourteen suggest a strong capacity for mindfulness.

Exhibit 4.3. Assessing Your Firm's Tendency Toward Doubt, Inquiry, and Updating.

Respond *agree* or *disagree* with the following statements about your work unit, department, or organization.

Doubt

1. People around here are quick to deny problems when they show up. _____

2. When someone voices a doubt or concern, people are quick to dismiss it. _____

3. When something unexpected occurs, we rarely try to figure out why things didn't go as we expected. _____

Inquiry

1. When something unexpected happens, the information is not widely shared. _____

2. When unexpected problems arise, those involved rarely spend time to debrief what they saw and heard prior to the incident. _____

3. When things don't go as expected, people rarely try to uncover what they assumed in the first place. _____

4. It is uncommon to check our assumptions against reality. _____

Updating

1. If things don't go as we expected, it is uncommon for people to update their original assumptions. _____

2. It is uncommon to revise our practices and procedures to incorporate revised assumptions and understandings. _____

Scoring: Count the number of *agree* and *disagree* responses. The greater the number of *agree* responses, the less the tendency to doubt, inquire, or update; hence, a greater potential for *mindlessness*. Use these questions to begin thinking of ways to improve your capacity for mindfulness.

of changes. If there appears to be a shortfall in the rudiments of mindfulness, it would make sense to give doubt, inquiry, and updating a more conspicuous and valued place in meeting agendas, performance appraisals, mentoring, socialization, and briefings. This way people will get used to these activities, get better at doing them, and be able to connect the accomplishment of these activities to improved outcomes.

■ Where You Need to Be Most Mindful

You need to be alert to the dimensions of mindfulness and mindlessness and how they permeate your work and your system. But you also need to be more attentive to situations where mindfulness can make a big difference. By that we mean situations where "ugly" surprises might be more likely to show up. Yale sociologist Charles Perrow suggests that unexpected events that can lead to failures or crises are most likely to occur in contexts that are *tightly coupled* and *interactively complex.*[7] *Coupling* concerns the degree to which actions in one part of the system directly and immediately affect other parts. A loosely coupled system is one where delays are possible and alternative pathways to completion are possible. A tightly coupled system has little slack and is one in which a process or set of activities, once initiated, proceeds rapidly and irreversibly to a known or unknown conclusion. Tightly coupled systems have more time-dependent processes, so items must move continuously through the production process, and delays or storage of incomplete products are not possible.[8] For example, nuclear power generation is a highly time-dependent and precise process, as is chemical processing.

Interactive complexity concerns how the different components or parts interact. For example, in a linear system such as an assembly line, components only interact with the other components that precede or follow in some direct sequence. Moreover, the assembly process is relatively well understood. If a belt breaks and the line stops, the problem is, relatively speaking, visible and comprehensible. Interactively complex systems possess a more elaborate set of interconnections and nonlinear feedback loops, some of which are hidden or impossible to anticipate. For example, nuclear power generation is not a set of independent, serial steps. Instead, it requires the coordination of numerous mechanical components by many operators. And despite years of operation, not all aspects of nuclear physics are completely understood.[9]

The rise of interconnected technologies, interconnected resource demands, and increased demands on attention mean that some parts of most organizational systems at one time or another move toward an interactively complex, tightly coupled state. Although mindfulness can't comprehend the incomprehensible, it can aid in the detection of early anomalies that can spiral into seemingly impossible outcomes. If you get a feel for whether your system is loosely or tightly coupled and linear or interactively complex, you may then be in a better position to know just how great the risk is of something unexpected and disastrous happening. If you have a tightly coupled, interactively complex system, you need to work on mindfulness. And soon.

Human factors psychologist James Reason provides an alternative view for assessing where unforeseen events will surface. Reason suggests that surprises are most likely to occur at the human-system interface and says that to assess this, managers should ask three questions:[10]

1. The "hands on" question: What activities involve the most direct human contact with the system and thus offer the greatest opportunity for human decisions or actions to have an immediate, direct, adverse effect upon the system?

2. The "criticality" question: What activities, if performed less than adequately, pose the greatest risks to the well-being of the system?
3. The "frequency" question: How often are these activities performed in the day-to-day operation of the system as a whole?

If an activity (or unit) scores "high" on all three of these questions, it is more likely to be vulnerable to unexpected events. Maintenance-related work, for example, scores high on all three criteria, and evidence from a number of studies supports the idea that maintenance either generates or extinguishes unexpected problems of some sort. In more mindful organizations, maintenance departments become central locations for organizational learning. Maintenance workers encounter failures at earlier stages of development and have an increased awareness of vulnerabilities in the technology, sloppiness in the operations, gaps in the procedures, and dependencies among problems.

Although maintenance workers may not be central in your organization, there are probably parallel positions or units in which early signs of failure are especially visible. For example, people who work with warranty returns, customer service, and tech support hot lines often come into contact with surprises that shed light on an organization's weaknesses. In addition to answering the questions in Exhibit 4.4, spend time to determine who in the organization makes observations equivalent to maintenance. Answers to these questions will give you an edge as you develop a better sense of where your system is most vulnerable.

■ Spotting Processes of Mindfulness in Your Organization

Up to this point, you have examined tendencies toward mindfulness and conditions where you might need it. The next part of the audit focuses on the five processes of mindfulness and probes your firm's current state with respect to preoccupation

Exhibit 4.4. Assessing Where Mindfulness Is Most Required.

Respond *agree* or *disagree* with the following statements about your work unit, department, or organization.

1. Work is accomplished through a number of sequential steps carried out in a linear fashion. _____

2. Feedback and information on what is happening is direct and simply verified. _____

3. The work process is relatively well understood and easily comprehensible. _____

4. The work process *does not require* coordinated action by numerous mechanical components and operators. _____

5. We can directly observe all the components in our "production" process. _____

6. Our work process is such that it is possible to put the system on a stand-by mode, and delays are possible because unfinished products or services can sit for a while or be stored without damage. _____

7. There are many ways to produce our product or service, items can be rerouted, schedules changed, and parts can be added later if delays or shortages occur. _____

8. There is a lot of slack in our work process and it does not require much precision; things don't have to be done right the first time because they can always be repeated. _____

9. There is a lot of opportunity to improvise when things go wrong. _____

Scoring: Count the number of *agree* and *disagree* responses. The greater the number of *disagree* responses, the more your system is interactively complex and tightly coupled, and therefore the more important it is be mindful. Use these questions to begin thinking of ways to improve your capacity for mindfulness.

with failure, reluctance to simplify, sensitivity to operations, commitment to resilience, and deference to expertise. When you look for these HRO processes in your firm, you are looking at the capability of your system to generate reliable mindfulness.

Preoccupation with Failure

Failure in an HRO can be more catastrophic than is true for failure in your firm. Despite this difference in magnitude, the diagnostic value of failure is similar in both settings. In either setting, failure means that there was a lapse in detection: Something was not caught as soon as it could have been caught. And it means that the system is not as healthy as it could be. An organization that is ignorant about failure, its location, genesis, and trajectory, is less mindful than it could be. But this deficiency need not be permanent. You can help the system be more alert to its failures, and you can do something about how the system handles failures and failure reporting. You can, for instance, help call attention to failure, articulate the consequences of continued denial of failure, uncover what happens to people when they report failures, seek similar failures elsewhere and benchmark how people manage them, spot the potential for failures in apparent successes, propose measures to detect failure systematically, and transmit memorable stories that preserve the lessons learned from failure. All these changes increase the capability for mindfulness.

Exhibit 4.5 can help you probe the degree to which your organization has a healthy preoccupation with failure. In doing this kind of mini-audit, you are also assessing the degree to which people are aware of mindfulness as a desirable outcome and of how it can be operationalized (for example, you notice how much time and effort people spend to understand a dynamic context). When it comes to mindfulness, it's good to feel bad, and bad to feel good. This inverted logic derives from the

Exhibit 4.5. Assessing Your Firm's Preoccupation with Failure.

How well do each of the following statements describe your work unit, department, or organization? Enter next to each item below the number that corresponds with your conclusion: 1 = not at all, 2 = to some extent, 3 = a great deal.

1. We focus more on our failures than our successes.   _____

2. We regard close calls and near misses as a kind of failure
   that reveals potential danger rather than as evidence of our
   success and ability to avoid disaster.   _____

3. We treat near misses and errors as information about the
   health of our system and try to learn from them.   _____

4. We often update our procedures after experiencing a close
   call or near miss to incorporate our new experience and
   enriched understanding.   _____

5. We make it hard for people to hide mistakes of any kind.   _____

6. People are inclined to report mistakes that have significant
   consequences even if nobody notices.   _____

7. Managers seek out and encourage bad news.   _____

8. People feel free to talk to superiors about problems.   _____

9. People are rewarded if they spot problems, mistakes, errors,
   or failures.   _____

Scoring: Add the numbers. If you score lower than eleven, you are preoccupied with *success* and should be actively considering how you can immediately improve your focus on *failure*. If you score between eleven and eighteen, you have a moderate preoccupation with success rather than a fully mindful preoccupation with failure. Scores higher than eighteen suggest a healthy preoccupation with failure and a strong capacity for mindfulness.

many dangers of complacency that accompany success. To feel good may be to relax attentiveness and allow problems to accumulate undetected.

Reluctance to Simplify

Part of what distinguishes high reliability organizations from other organizations is the extent to which they obsess about the question of what they ignore. But this difference is beginning to disappear. As turbulent global environments have become increasingly hard to anticipate and surprise has become more common, organizations of all kinds have become more mindful of what they ignore and more eager to learn how they can alter their processes of simplification. Their wariness and concern with blind spots is beginning to match the routine skepticism of HROs.

When you seek out the reluctance to simplify in your organization, you want to find how the system socializes people to make fewer assumptions, notice more, and ignore less. Probes into simplifications such as those presented in Exhibit 4.6 are probes into the existence of norms that acknowledge the reality of surprise and convey messages such as *take nothing for granted* and *don't get into something without a way out*. But those items also assess the capability to look outside the confines of current expectations, to question and restrain temptations to simplify—capabilities cultivated by a requisite variety in human thought and action. Requisite variety is encouraged through diverse checks and balances that come from adversarial reviews, committees and meetings, frequent job rotation and retraining, and the selection of employees with nontypical prior experience.

Divergence in viewpoints provides the group with a broader set of assumptions and sensitivity to a greater variety of inputs, both of which are the antithesis of simplification. Unfortunately, diverse views typically are disproportionately distributed toward the bottom of the organization, which means that those most

Exhibit 4.6. Assessing Your Firm's Reluctance to Simplify.

How well do each of the following statements describe your work unit, department, or organization? Enter next to each item below the number that corresponds with your conclusion: 1 = not at all, 2 = to some extent, 3 = a great deal.

1. People around here take nothing for granted. _____

2. Questioning is encouraged. _____

3. We strive to challenge the status quo. _____

4. People in this organization feel free to bring up problems and tough issues. _____

5. People generally prolong their analysis to better grasp the nature of the problems that come up. _____

6. People are encouraged to express different views of the world. _____

7. People listen carefully; it is rare that anyone's view is dismissed. _____

8. People are not shot down for surfacing information that could interrupt operations. _____

9. When something unexpected happens, people are more concerned with listening and conducting a complete analysis of the situation than with advocating for their view. _____

10. We appreciate skeptics. _____

11. People demonstrate trust for each other. _____

12. People show a great deal of mutual respect for each other. _____

Scoring: Add the numbers. If you score higher than twenty-four, the potential to *avoid simplification* is strong. If you score between fourteen and twenty-four, the potential to avoid simplification is moderate. Scores lower than fourteen suggest that you should actively be considering how you can immediately improve your capabilities to prevent simplification in order to improve your firm's capacity for mindfulness.

likely to catch unanticipated warning signals have the least power and argumentative skill to persuade others that the signal should be taken seriously. This isn't fatal if interpersonal skills and mutual respect are valued and if bullheadedness, hubris, and self-importance are not. Skeptics, curmudgeons, iconoclasts all are welcome in a mindful system, even if their presence is a bit of a pain. But this welcoming attitude exists only if there is strong shared sentiment that mindfulness is imperative to success. Short of that consensus, skeptics can have a rough time and find themselves dismissed with speed and enthusiasm.

Sensitivity to Operations

HROs are less concerned with strategy, which we conventionally equate with the big picture of the future, than with the big picture in the moment. Diagnosing your firm's sensitivity to operations by probing into the directions set out in Exhibit 4.7 can help you appraise how prepared you are to avert the accumulation of small events that can grow into bigger problems.

Being sensitive to operations is a unique way to correct failures of foresight. A comprehensive view of current operations enables organizations to catch most of the small errors and mistakes that would normally go unnoticed and be left to cumulate. By keeping errors from accumulating, the readiness to make large numbers of small adjustments reduces the likelihood that any one error will become aligned with another and interact with it in ways not previously anticipated.

You can help your system be more sensitive to operations by appraising the extent to which leaders and managers maintain continuous contact with the operating system or front line and the extent to which they are accessible when important situations develop. To what extent is there ongoing group interaction and information sharing about actual operations and workplace characteristics?

Exhibit 4.7. Assessing Your Firm's Sensitivity to Operations.

Respond *agree* or *disagree* with the following statements about your organization.

1. On a day-to-day basis, there is an ongoing presence of someone who is paying attention to what is happening and is readily available for consultation if something unexpected arises. _____

2. Should problems occur, someone with the authority to act is always accessible and available, especially to people on the front lines. _____

3. Supervisors readily pitch in whenever necessary. _____

4. During an average day, people come into enough contact with each other to build a clear picture of the current situation. _____

5. People are always looking for feedback about things that aren't going right. _____

6. People are familiar with operations beyond one's own job. _____

7. We have access to resources if unexpected surprises crop up. _____

8. Managers constantly monitor workloads and are able to obtain additional resources if the workload starts to become excessive. _____

Scoring: Count the number of *agree* and *disagree* responses. The greater the number of *disagree* responses, the less the *sensitivity to operations*. Use these questions to begin thinking of ways to improve your sensitivity to operations and capacity for mindfulness.

Commitment to Resilience

The central tension in the HRO literature is that once a mistake starts to amplify in a system, that error may be the system's last trial. So people in HROs try to do everything they can to anticipate possible failure modes. The reality, of course, is that humans and technologies are fallible. HROs accept the inevitability of error. This acceptance shifts attention from the ideal of error prevention to the more realistic goal of error containment.

Like HROs, your organization probably tries to prevent or anticipate surprises, but equally important is the question, How well prepared is your system to *manage* the unexpected when it does happen? We focus on the word *manage* to make it clear that people deal with surprises not only by anticipation that weeds them out in advance but also by resilience that responds to them as they occur. Resilience is about bouncing back from errors and about coping with surprises in the moment. The capability for resilience, even if it is not exercised, aids diagnosis and detection of unwarranted simplifications and a cumulative trend in a series of errors. It is achieved through the use of expert networks, an extensive action repertoire, and skills with improvisation—resources that are probed in Exhibit 4.8. Probes into your firm's commitment to resilience are probes into learning, knowledge, and capability development. Earlier in this chapter we suggested that a major source of limited perception is a limited action repertoire. Expanding people's general knowledge and technical capabilities improves their abilities both to see problems in the making and to deal with them. Commitment to resilience is also evident in a capacity to use knowledge in unexpected ways. This capacity in your organization might be evident in informal networks of people who self-organize to solve problems, in enthusiasm to share expertise and novel solutions across unit boundaries, and in continual investments in improving technical systems, procedures, reporting processes, and employee attentiveness.

Exhibit 4.8. Assessing Your Firm's Commitment to Resilience.

How well do each of the following statements describe your work unit, department, or organization? Enter next to each item below the number that corresponds with your conclusion: 1 = not at all, 2 = to some extent, 3 = a great deal.

1. Forecasting and predicting the future is not that important here. _____

2. Resources are continually devoted to training and retraining people on the properties of the technical system. _____

3. People have more than enough training and experience for the kind of work they have to do. _____

4. This organization is actively concerned with developing people's skills and knowledge. _____

5. This organization encourages challenging stretch assignments. _____

6. People around here are known for their ability to use their knowledge in novel ways. _____

7. There is a concern with building people's competence and response repertoires. _____

8. People have a number of informal contacts that they sometimes use to solve problems. _____

9. People learn from their mistakes. _____

10. People are able to rely on others. _____

Scoring: Add the numbers. If you score higher than twenty, the *commitment to resilience* is strong. If you score between twelve and twenty, the commitment to resilience is moderate. Scores lower than twelve suggest that you should actively consider how you can immediately begin building resilience and the capacity for mindfulness.

Deference to Expertise

In our analysis of high reliability organizing in Chapter Three, we confronted the paradox that the adoption of orderly procedures to reduce unexpected problems sometimes makes those problems worse. In the face of such a possibility and in response to changes in the tempo of demands, HROs shift their decision dynamics, authority structures, and functional patterns. There is a growing recognition that all organizations will require the same potential for flexible response if they are to cope with diverse and rapidly changing competitive circumstances.

An audit of the extent to which your firm defers to expertise is more than a simple assessment of delegation or the extent to which decision rights are disseminated to people lower down in the hierarchy. It is a deeper probe into the extent to which people structure their attention. Recall from Chapter Three that effective HROs enact a more flexible decision-making structure when something goes wrong. What they do is loosen the designation of who the "important" decision maker is in order to allow decision making and problems to migrate to the person or team with expertise in that choice-problem combination. Recall also that decisions migrate down as well as up. When tasks are highly interdependent and time is compressed, decisions migrate down to people at the point of problem sensing. Decisions migrate up when events are unique or have political or career ramifications that require organizational experience or familiarity that is more often found at higher than lower levels. Probes into your firm's deference to expertise are probes into accountability, responsibility, and broad awareness of where to go for help. Probing in the directions captured in Exhibit 4.9 provides a more systematic appraisal of the deference to expertise in your organization and should give you insight into your capability to localize problems and limit their spread.

Exhibit 4.9. Assessing the Deference to Expertise in Your Firm.

How well do each of the following statements describe your work unit, department, or organization? Enter next to each item below the number that corresponds with your conclusion: 1 = not at all, 2 = to some extent, 3 = a great deal.

1. People are committed to doing their job well.   _____

2. People respect the nature of one another's job activities.   _____

3. If something out of the ordinary happens, people know who has the expertise to respond.   _____

4. People in this organization value expertise and experience over hierarchical rank.   _____

5. In this organization, the people most qualified to make decisions make them.   _____

6. If something unexpected occurs, the most highly qualified people, regardless of rank, make the decisions.   _____

7. People typically "own" a problem until it is resolved.   _____

8. It is generally easy for us to obtain expert assistance when something comes up that we don't know how to handle.   _____

Scoring: Add the numbers. If you score higher than sixteen, the *deference to expertise* is strong. If you score between ten and sixteen, the deference to expertise is moderate. Scores lower than ten suggest that you should actively think of ways to improve the deference to expertise and capacity for mindfulness.

■ Interpreting the Audit and Using the Results

An audit usually stirs up a system. When you ask questions such as those presented in this chapter, people begin to pay attention to the issues implied by the questions. They talk about these topics. They refine their answers. They find themselves saying, "I wish I'd said . . ." It's pretty hard not to have these extended reactions when your attention has been drawn to a topic.

By their very nature, then, audits help create readiness. But readiness for what? In our case, there are several answers. First, the audit should help you get more comfortable with the unexpected because it has become increasingly common. Second, it should provide a motive to benchmark on an unfamiliar organization, the high reliability organization (HRO), which relies heavily on mindfulness to manage the unexpected and maintain relatively error-free performance. And finally, it should help you increase your capability for mindfulness as a means to manage the unexpected. If we embedded our discussion in the current "hot topics" of business, we would simply note that those consultants who go on and on about speed as the new imperative in organizations are really talking about a special case of the unexpected. In our view, if you increase your capability for mindfulness, speed will take care of itself. So we want you to feel more willing to grapple with the unexpected rather than avoid it, more willing to grapple with the unexpected mindfully rather than mindlessly, and more willing to benchmark on HROs as the teachers of how to deal mindfully with the unexpected. By undertaking the audit, particularly if many people are part of the process, you can help enlarge your organization's mindfulness about its mindful qualities.

We encourage you to answer the questions posed in the audit and then ask others in your company to do the same. But before you talk to people at different hierarchical levels, functions, specialties, and locations within your firm about the results, we want you to go one step further. We encourage you to estimate *in advance* answers for the other units, functions, specialties, and locations within your own organization (ask them to do the same for you) and then compare your answers with theirs. When you exchange your observations, you will generate a richer picture of your system as you seek to understand the reasons for differences in your observations. How did you answer the questions posed in the audit? How did others answer the questions posed in the audit? To what extent did your assessment of other units match their assessment and vice versa? What did you not find that you expected to find? What did you find that you did not expect to find? What surprised you? Remember the importance of surprise. Feelings of surprise are diagnostic because they are a solid cue that one's model of the world is flawed.

When you evaluate the responses to the audit items, look at four issues. First, to what extent do people's assessments match across your organization? In the best case, similarities in responses across hierarchical levels, units, and functions will give you an integrated big picture similar to that found in the best-prepared HROs; in the worst case, the emerging picture will be fragmented, with people at certain levels, in particular functions or units giving answers that suggest they have a rich set of mindful processes in place and others giving answers that suggest mindlessness is more the norm. You probably show tendencies toward mindlessness and toward mindfulness. Now, do you exhibit them at the *"right"* places? Are you mindless toward environments that are stable and predictable, and mindful in environments that are dynamic and unpredictable?

Look for items with high variation of the scores. This means people do not agree on that characteristic of the work unit, department, or organization. Where answers differ, consider the reasons for these differences and their implications. Disagreement often is a signal that something is being overlooked. So it is worthwhile to air the reasons for these differences in opinion because those with different ideas may have insights that no one else has. What is important is to get these differences into the open, especially if people provide credible evidence in support of their assessment. That clears the air of wishful thinking.

Second, what are you good at? Are you consistently better at anticipation (the first three processes of mindfulness) than containment (last two processes)? You would expect that to occur in rational organizations, obsessed with planning. And because the value of building resilience and developing flexible decision processes is often underestimated in most organizations, it is natural to expect the latter two processes to be your poorest. Are they? If not, you're on your way to being a more mindful organization. Rank order the five processes according to what you are best and worst at doing. Is your culture what is holding that rank ordering in place? Compare the rankings written by the top-most persons in the hierarchy with those written by the bottom-most persons in the hierarchy. Does the top see what the bottom sees? Is bad news reaching the top? Is there unexpected good news? Is the organization actually more mindful than the top believes? Tell them.

Which unit, function, or department appears to be higher performing on each of the five processes? Pay particular attention to units that seem to have scored well, since this can signal a unit or department that has learned some important lessons about how to achieve mindfulness—lessons that can be shared with the rest of the firm.

Third, what is dismaying? Ask your coworkers what dismayed and alarmed them when they saw the results. If nothing is dismaying or alarming, ask yourself why not? The lack of dismay could be a sign of deadly complacency with the status quo and could represent a major barrier to enacting a more mindful infrastructure.

Finally, look carefully at the specific items that indicate your work unit, department, or organization is not as mindful as it could be. Use the survey results to diagnose areas that need specific attention and formulate an action plan. As a group decide what you can do to improve the capacity for mindfulness. Look to other groups or units that appear to have mastered the process for help in deciding on a course of action (we will introduce specific remedies in the following two chapters from which you can choose). Assign a champion for the process. Once you decide what you want to change, you also need to determine how progress on these fronts will be measured—change in what? What is a significant time interval in which to see some change? Make sure that someone is appointed to monitor and report progress on accomplishing any change to your mindful infrastructure.

When should people in your group repeat the audit? You can use the items included in the audit as part of an ongoing monitoring process and of course should add additional items as your experience and understanding of your system grows. For example, pick a failure-of-the-month to scrutinize. Assess where you stand on the processes as you work your way through your analysis. What happens the next month as a consequence of treating the first failure more mindfully? Slippage (which occurs as scores start to change in the untoward direction) can indicate a drift away from mindfulness and can signal areas that may need attention and reinforcement.

People in HROs spend the bulk of their time re-accomplishing and reinforcing efforts to build a mindful infrastructure. They understand that mindful processes unravel pretty fast. The uncertain technology and environment warrants nothing less than an ongoing effort. We believe that the same holds true for you. In today's context it makes sense for any organization to become more like an HRO. Today's business conditions involve increased competition, higher customer expectations, reduced cycle time, and tight interdependencies. These changes produce environments that are almost as harsh, risky, and unforgiving as those that HROs confront. That being the case, organizations that confront an HRO-like environment with HRO-like processes should have more success at learning and adaptation than those who don't.

CHAPTER SUMMARY

In this chapter we have converted the lessons learned from the study of high reliability organizations into sets of questions to help you assess your firm's mindfulness, tendencies toward mindlessness, and current infrastructure to combat mindlessness. We suggested that you customize the audit for your unique context and administer it widely. The information you gain from administering the audit across hierarchies, specialties, and functions is a prime source of information about what people know about their system, the ways in which it can fail, and the defenses in place to prevent surprises from getting out of hand.

Implicit in this discussion were some suggestions for how you can begin to institutionalize mindfulness and the set of processes that contribute to it. Of course, there are many techniques that relate directly or indirectly to managing unexpected events, such as effective people-management practices, selection, training, skill checks, design of procedures, and administrative mechanisms. It is not within the scope of this book to review all possible techniques. Rather, our focus is on operating practices that relate directly to the five elements that create a mindful infrastructure and enable HROs to be more aware of their own capabilities, what they face, and what that might mean. The next two chapters further develop these ideas.

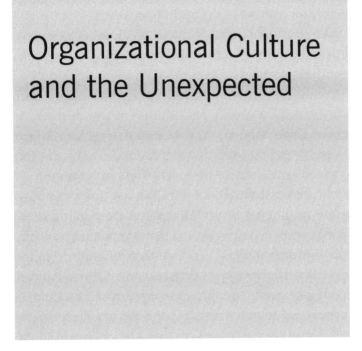

Organizational Culture and the Unexpected

The brief period after you have finished the mindfulness audit is a lot like the time right after the chaos of battle on the battlefield. There are truths lying around everywhere that may be picked up for the asking. These are the moments of learning. But it won't be long before moments of candor give way to moments of normalizing that protect reputations, decisions, and styles of managing. After the unexpected occurs, the minute official stories get "straightened out" and repeated, learning stops. The same is likely to be true of the moments of truth stirred up by an audit of mindfulness. HROs manage to stretch those moments. And you can do the same. That's the purpose of these final two chapters. We want you to hold onto the candid audit of mindfulness in your group long enough to see ways to improve on what the audit uncovered.

Let's take stock of where you will be as soon as you've completed the mindfulness audit. You've seen the Union Pacific Railroad mindlessly bungle a merger and endanger people in doing so. You've seen that expectations impose substantial blinders that are removed only by continuous, mindful efforts that counteract misperceptions. You've seen that mindfulness is about updating to get the situation right. You've audited your own group to see how it stacks up in its efforts to act mindfully and to enact processes that achieve mindfulness. You've spotted some attitudes and behavior that keep you from being more mindful. In that sense, you've spotted symptoms that probably suggest that your organization is not all that different from the Union Pacific. But you've also spotted some attitudes and behaviors already present in your group that promote mindfulness and are more crucial to managing the unexpected than you realized. The chances are that you didn't realize they were so important. And neither did the other people in the group. So now you find yourself with a list of behaviors and processes to add, delete, and reaffirm.

What you need to do next is modify what people expect from one another by way of mindful updating. This modification is not just a change in how people *think,* as important as that is, but it is also a change in how they *feel.* You need people to absorb the lessons of mindfulness at an emotional level so that they will express approval when others hold certain beliefs and act in certain ways. For example, people need to feel strongly that it's good to speak up when they make a mistake, good to spot flawed assumptions, good to focus on a persistent operational anomaly. They need to expect praise for these acts when they do them, and they need to offer praise when they spot someone else doing them. Likewise, you need to attach disapproval to people believing and acting in ways that undermine mindfulness. For example, people need to agree among themselves and feel strongly that it's bad to refrain from asking for help, bad to let success go to their heads, bad to ignore lower-ranking experts. They need to express key values by making clear what is disapproved as much as by praising what is approved.

When people make these kinds of changes, a new culture begins to emerge. The culture takes the form of a new set of expectations and a new urgency that people live up to them. In the case of mindfulness, they start living up to the expectation that everyone in the organization should work mindfully, that there are no exceptions, and that those who think otherwise will be nudged from the center of the group to the periphery. An organizational culture emerges from a set of expectations that matter to people. Powerful social forces such as inclusion, exclusion, praise, positive feelings, social support, isolation, care, indifference, excitement, and anger are the means by which people make things matter for one another. We're talking about norms, values, consensus, and intensity, all of which make up corporate culture. All of us are products of our relationships, our mutual accommodations with other people, and the respectful interactions that define us. This means that cultures shape us: They pull behaviors from us that we are more or less proud of, draw attention to certain values and away from other ones, and influence our priorities.

This chapter is about what holds your group together, what gives it its prevailing tone, and what needs to be changed if mindfulness is to be institutionalized and sustained. True, the only person you can change is yourself. Moreover, you "alone" can become more mindful and champion these behaviors, model them, and benefit from them in a limited way. (We focus on these close-in, personal implications in Chapter Six.) But prevailing cultures shape you and how your acts are interpreted. This means that even the best-intentioned small pockets of mindful action can get swept away by prevailing, socially approved mindlessness.

You'll see an example of this when we discuss the Moura mine disaster. If, however, you get the culture right, if people begin to agree that mindfulness leads to more reliable outcomes and more predictability, and if people begin to expect mindfulness from one another and approve those who take mindfulness seriously and disapprove those who don't, you will be moving toward a set of norms that hold mindfulness in place and make it the prevailing tone among your associates. And that, in turn, will make it a whole lot easier for you personally to model more of the subtleties of mindful action that you picked up while reflecting on the mindfulness audit. That's why we look first at culture.

In the remainder of this chapter we first lay out an overview of what we mean by culture, noting especially its close affinity to the idea of expectations: In brief, culture is both a way of seeing and a way of not seeing. Second, we translate the general picture of culture into a more specific picture that is focused on mindfulness by exploring James Reason's notion of an informed safety culture. We show how an informed culture is designed to augment mindfulness. And we show, using the example of the Moura mine disaster, how a less mindful, less informed culture mismanages the unexpected with fatal results. We conclude with a detailed set of guidelines for reshaping your existing culture toward greater valuing of mindfulness.

■ Properties of Corporate Culture

One of the earliest discussions of organizational culture, Barry Turner's work in the early 1970s, remains one of the clearest descriptions of culture and its importance for organizing. In Turner's words: "Part of the effectiveness of organizations lies in the way in which they are able to bring together large numbers of people and imbue them for a sufficient time with a sufficient similarity of approach, outlook and priorities to enable them to achieve collective, sustained responses which would be impossible if a group of unorganized individuals were to face the same problem. However, this very property also brings with it the dangers of a collective blindness to important issues, the danger that some vital factors may be left outside the bounds of organizational perception."[1]

In other words, culture is the source of blind spots. It is also the source of an economical, powerful "similarity of approach." This similarity results from shared values, norms, and perceptions that are the raw materials of culture. When these raw materials are held in common, the resulting "shared expectations associated with clusters of roles in an organizational group tend to encourage members of the group to bring certain assumptions to the task of decision making within the organization, and to operate with similar views of rationality."[2] It is these shared expectations, assumptions, and similar views of rationality that can either encourage or discourage mindfulness.

Key Properties of Culture

Of the many recent descriptions that attempt to capture key properties of cultures, Edgar Schein's is perhaps the best known.[3] He says that "culture is defined by six formal properties: (1) shared basic assumptions that are (2) invented, discovered, or developed by a given group as it (3) learns to cope with its problem of external adaptation and internal integration in ways that (4) have worked well enough to be considered valid, and, therefore, (5) can be taught to new members of the group as the (6) correct way to perceive, think, and feel in relation to those problems." When we talk about culture, therefore, we are talking about *assumptions* that preserve lessons learned from dealing with the outside and the inside; *values* derived from these assumptions that prescribe how the organization should act; and *artifacts* or visible markers and activities that embody and give substance to the espoused values. Artifacts are the easiest to change, assumptions the hardest. If top management sends down an order that subordinates will be empowered, but in practice subordinates continue to seek permission for their actions, this contradiction is a clear signal that a basic assumption is operating, in this case the assumption that hierarchy always matters.

What Schein has spelled out in careful detail, most people spell out much more compactly: Culture is how we do things around here. For our purposes we modify that slightly and argue that *culture is what we expect around here.* Cultures affect both what people expect from one another (these expectations are often called norms) and what people expect from their dealings with the external environment of customers, competitors, suppliers, shareholders, and so on.[4] In either case expectations take the form of agreements about appropriate attitudes and behaviors. What differs from group to group are the extent to which people agree on what is appropriate and how strongly they feel about the appropriateness of the attitude or behavior. If everyone feels strongly about the importance of a behavior, there is little latitude for deviation, and slight departures from the norm are dealt with swiftly and harshly. For instance, if a group of commuter pilots feel strongly that checklists are for the weak and lame, anyone who even so much as mentions the word *checklist* or tries to use one unobtrusively is likely to be sanctioned by ridicule or frowns of disapproval. If, however, agreement is less widespread and people feel less passionate about the issue, there is a weaker norm around checklists, deviations are more commonplace, and the culture itself will do little to hold the group together in this respect.

How Culture Develops

Here's an example of how culture develops. Dennis Bakke, CEO of AES (a global power-generation company), made the following comment to a reporter from *Fast Company* magazine: "Specialization is the root of a lot of boredom. Talented specialists tend to dumb down the rest of the organization [AES has 40,000 employees]. As soon as you have a specialist who's very good, everyone else quits thinking. The better the person is, the worse it is for the organization. All the education flows to the person who already knows the most."[5]

That view of specialization is a key assumption made by top people at AES. It represents one of Bakke's beliefs about how life unfolds in the organization. More important, it represents a belief about how life *should* unfold in AES, so that view is also a value. People at AES should be generalists rather than specialists. This value becomes treated as a norm when it begins to affect who gets selected and rejected for employment and how they are treated once they join AES. People in AES are treated as "mini-CEOs," all 40,000 are treated as "insiders" by the Securities Exchange Commission (SEC) because of their access to information, and all 40,000 are fair game for assignment to projects in which they may have little expertise, projects such as investing cash reserves or making deals to supply power for long periods. If people plunge into these projects, seek input from varied sources, and are fully engaged, these are appropriate behaviors and people get approval even if they make occasional mistakes. People who make no mistakes but who behave in a less engaged, more detached manner are acting inappropriately and are the targets of widespread disapproval. To be fully engaged in an organization's work is to meet expectations and to take seriously a value that everyone else takes seriously. In the case of AES this value is *fun,* which to insiders means having total responsibility for decisions and being accountable for results, regardless of one's level in the firm.

How Culture Controls

The key point to remember about values, culture, and expectations was first mentioned two decades ago by Thomas Peters and Robert Waterman in their best-seller *In Search of Excellence.*

They argued that if people in an organization were committed to no more than three or four core values and if they internalized these values and shared them, top management could give these committed people wide latitude to make decisions because they would frame those decisions in a similar, preferred manner. The handful of key values would shape how people perceived an issue and how they acted. Hence, an organization could gain the benefits of both centralization and decentralization if members were centralized on a handful of key values and then given autonomy on everything else. Peters and Waterman stated the point this way: "Autonomy is a product of discipline. The discipline ([instilled by] a few shared values) provides the framework. It gives people confidence (to experiment for instance) stemming from stable expectations about what really counts. . . . [T]he discipline of a small number of shared values induces practical autonomy and experimentation throughout the organization."[6] A culture with three or four key values that have been converted into norms for appropriate behavior, norms that are shared widely and implemented with intensity, will be coordinated, resilient, opportunistic.

Hence, culture is a key element in efforts to manage the unexpected mindfully. That assertion is both simple and quite complex. It is simple in the sense that the idea of culture itself is simple: "There is nothing magical or elusive about corporate culture. One has only to be clear about the specific attitudes and behaviors that are desired, and then to identify the norms or expectations that promote or impede them."[7] But culture is also quite complex. Figure 5.1 shows that there are many conditions that have to fall into place in order to produce clear norms and a strong culture. In particular, a culture of mindfulness, animated by norms of appropriate behavior, is likely *if* top management conveys a clear preference for mindfulness in its beliefs, values, and actions; *if* those actions and words are communicated credibly and consistently and remain salient for everyone; *if* those communicated values are seen to be consistent rather

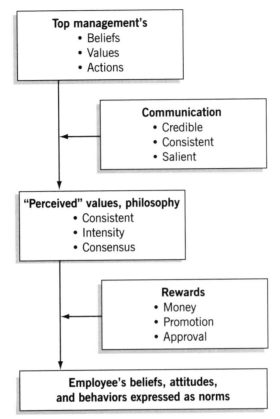

Figure 5.1. Conditions That Create Corporate Culture.

than hypocritical and are felt strongly by the majority of people; and *if* bonuses, raises, promotions, and approval flow toward those who act mindfully and away from those who don't. That is a lot of *ifs*. And those *ifs* represent lots of places where efforts to build a strong, mindful culture can get sidetracked.

How Culture Is Changed

Culture change is hard, slow, and subject to frequent relapse. We think that culture researcher Edgar Schein is absolutely right when he counsels people to attempt culture change only when there is a specific problem to be solved and only when they can work with existing cultural strengths. He makes the point this way:

> Never start with the idea of changing culture. Always start with the issue the organization faces; only when those business issues are clear should you ask yourself whether the culture aids or hinders resolving the issues. Always think initially of the culture as your source of strength. It is the residue of your past successes. Even if some elements of the culture look dysfunctional, remember that they are probably only a few among a large set of others that continue to be strengths. If changes need to be made in how the organization is run, try to build on existing cultural strengths rather than attempting to change those elements that may be weaknesses.[8]

When you filled out the mindfulness audit in Chapter Four, chances are you found some business issues you may need to resolve and some positive cultural features that you can exploit in doing so. For example, you may have discovered that your work unit, executive team, or organization

- Makes too many mistakes
- Is too unreliable
- Gets interrupted too often
- Intercepts problems too late
- Is the last to spot changes
- Perennially plays catch up
- Limps from one near miss to another
- Is slow to learn
- Loses experts to competitors
- Makes things worse more often than making them better
- Is beset with any of a million other forms of unexpected events that persist and drain scarce resources

If your audit uncovered problems like these, a move toward a more mindful culture makes sense because it can resolve these kinds of issues. And if there are subgroups in your firm who already dissect their failures, complicate their simplifications, double-check their operations, pride themselves on swift reactions, and know where the experts are, you can build on their efforts. Don't waste your early efforts on those who hide failures, simplify, do strategy, anticipate, and give orders. Even if they stop doing those things, there is no guarantee that they will then start doing things that are more mindful.

Regardless of your circumstance, be sure to recognize that culture is a reality. Culture may further your agenda, or it may defeat it. But you can be sure that culture will affect what you see and how you interpret it. And those effects will determine whether you get the upper hand with the unexpected and learn and update your understanding based on your encounters with it.

■ Safety Culture as a Mindful Culture

The concept of safety culture illuminates what it means to create a culture of mindfulness. The term *safety culture* entered public awareness through the vocabulary of nuclear safety after the Chernobyl nuclear power plant explosion. The term has spread quickly to the commercial aviation and chemical processing industries. It is also prominent in the newly released and controversial report on the high incidence of "adverse medical events" in the health care system.[9] In the report on medical errors we read, for example, "Health care organizations must develop a culture of safety such that an organization's care processes and workforce are focused on improving the reliability and safety of care for patients."[10]

Descriptions of safety culture often read like lists of banal injunctions to "do good." James Reason, however, was able to find a description of safety culture that did not fall directly into this trap, and quoted it with some relief: "The safety culture of an organization is the product of individual and group values, attitudes, competencies, and patterns of behaviour that determine the commitment to, and the style and proficiency of, an organization's health and safety programmes. Organizations with a positive safety culture are characterized by communications founded on mutual trust, by shared perceptions of the importance of safety, and by confidence in the efficacy of preventive measures."[11]

Our interest in safety cultures stems first from their value as a way to illustrate the nature of corporate culture in general, second, from their concern with mindfulness, and third, from the fact that lapses in safe practice generate errors that produce unexpected events. Because culture, mindfulness, and coping with the unexpected are visible in safety cultures, they illustrate what it means to create a more mindful organization. Here we briefly examine one such formulation, James Reason's description of an informed culture, and show how adoption of some of its conditions might have prevented the Moura underground coal mine explosion on August 7, 1994, that killed eleven miners in Australia.

■ Safety Culture as an Informed Culture

Human factors researcher James Reason has developed a detailed and persuasive argument that a safety culture is an "informed culture."[12] An informed culture is "one in which those who manage and operate the system have current knowledge about the human, technical, organizational, and environmental factors that determine the safety of the system as a whole."[13] Reason worries most about events and entities that penetrate and breach an organization's defenses, so he pays close attention to whether a safety culture creates and sustains intelligent wariness. His data suggest that the best way to maintain these states of wariness is to collect and disseminate information about incidents, near misses, and the state of the system's vital signs.

The problem is that candid reporting of errors takes trust and trustworthiness. Both are hard to develop, easy to destroy, and hard to institutionalize. Reason argues that it takes four subcultures to ensure an informed culture. Assumptions, values, and artifacts must line up consistently around the issues of (1) what gets reported when people make errors or experience near misses (reporting culture); (2) how people apportion blame when something goes wrong (just culture); (3) how readily people can adapt to sudden and radical increments in pressure, pacing, and intensity (flexible culture); and (4) how adequately people can convert the lessons that they have learned into reconfigurations of assumptions, frameworks, and action (learning culture). All four are necessary for people to be informed and safe. And there were problems with all four subcultures in the Moura mine disaster.

Reporting Culture

Consider first a *reporting culture*. Since safety cultures are dependent on the knowledge gained from rare incidents, mistakes, near misses, and other "free lessons," they need to be structured so that people feel willing to "confess" their own errors. A reporting culture is about protection of people who report. And it is also about what kinds of reports are trusted. This is where the Moura mine disaster comes in.

The firm that operated the Moura mine, BHP, had as one of its basic cultural assumptions the idea that knowledge based on personal experience was the most trusted source of knowledge. People felt that such knowledge was easier to remember and more reliable.[14] The next most trusted source of knowledge was oral communication, and the least trusted source was written communication, such as reports filed after every shift in the mine. Those assumptions all seem pretty straightforward. But they worked together in a tragic way.

Prior to the mine explosion that killed eleven men, supervisors had reported in writing on several occasions that they smelled benzene. This was a sign that coal was heating and was moving toward a condition where spontaneous combustion could occur. Spontaneous combustion occurs at the same temperature as the ignition point for methane gas to explode. If there is a significant accumulation of methane gas when spontaneous combustion occurs, the mine explodes. This is what happened at Moura.

Senior officials ignored written reports that benzene smells were growing stronger. When shift supervisors talked to senior officials and mentioned the smells, the officials still didn't accept these reports but went down to see for themselves. They couldn't replicate the smell; this is not surprising, since warning signs of spontaneous combustion are intermittent, fleeting, and different for observers who check on them at different times. When the senior people smelled nothing, they dismissed both the written and oral reports of a strong benzene smell and attributed the odor instead to grease drums in the area. Soon thereafter the mine exploded. In a world where people assume that personal experience is primary, if the experience of a senior person does not detect a danger sensed by a junior person, the case is closed. The culture says so.

The scenario we have just sketched is a good example of the importance of keeping operations at the center of the big picture (the third process of mindfulness, *sensitivity to operations*). In the case of the Moura mine, the crucial question was, What is the current condition of the mine? The expert on that question (the fifth process, *deference to expertise*) is the person who has been working in that mine for an extended period, at the current coal face, who knows the smells of normal operations and has the big picture of the current situation. Simply because the administrators have more seniority does not mean that their experience is any more relevant; nor does it mean that their one-time sampling is any more valid than are the multiple samples taken by people who spend hours in the mine. But all that subtlety gets lost because of the simplified assumption that knowledge based on personal experience is what matters. The authorities smell nothing. So nothing exists. This all happens so swiftly, so neatly, so consensually, that we can better understand why HROs are so reluctant to simplify their assumptions and so eager to take almost nothing for granted. And we can better understand why a culture cannot be safe if its reports and reporting relationships are flawed.

Just Culture

An informed culture is also a *just culture.* An organization is defined by how it handles blame and punishment, and that in turn can affect what gets reported in the first place. A just culture is described as "an atmosphere of trust in which people are encouraged, even rewarded, for providing essential safety-related information—but in which they are clear about where the line must be drawn between acceptable and unacceptable behavior."[15] That line is crucial because it separates unacceptable behavior that deserves disciplinary action from acceptable behavior for which punishment is not appropriate and the potential for learning is considerable. It is impossible to do away with such a line altogether because "a culture in which all acts are immune from punishment would lack credibility in the eyes of the workforce."[16] Reason reports that when this line is clear, only about 10 percent of the unsafe acts actually fall into the "unacceptable" category.[17] This means that the other 90 percent are blameless and could be reported without fear of punishment. But if people are unclear about what constitutes grounds for punishment, if people feel ashamed to admit errors, and if management deals with errors in an inconsistent manner, then that 90 percent will be concealed. As a result, the system will be seriously deficient in understanding how vulnerable it really is.

Managers at the Moura mine contributed to mindlessness and danger because they withheld essential safety-related information and discouraged a just culture. The night of the mine explosion, management knew that the level of methane in a newly sealed area of the mine would begin to enter the explosive range shortly after 11:30 P.M. Sunday night.[18] They also knew that it would move out of the explosive range within two days. After two days there would not be enough oxygen left to ignite a fire. There was a short but lethal window of danger. "Management appeared simply to hope in some confused way that the sealed area would pass through the explosive range without ignition."[19] Management's hopes were fantasies. The mine exploded at 11:35 P.M., just five minutes after it was predicted to enter the explosive range.

What makes this an issue of a just culture is that there was a new shift of miners scheduled to go underground at 10:30 P.M. on Sunday night. The question was, should they be sent underground as scheduled or should they be kept out of the mine until it passed safely through the explosive range? Management did not wrestle directly with the question of whether the miners should go down, but instead wrestled with the question, What should be done if the men express any concerns about going down? The shift manager was told "not to raise the matter with the crews because if they had any concern they would raise it themselves." The miners didn't raise the matter because they had not been told that a nearby coal panel had been sealed off abruptly the night before due to a strong tar smell and haze. Management felt it wasn't necessary to give a briefing to the miners "because the men were well aware of the situation as it was."[20] But the miners weren't aware. They assumed that if there were any danger they would be told.

Technically, the miners weren't forced underground and the decision to go down was theirs. But they had no idea that they were making a "decision" to enter an unsafe mine. Andrew Hopkins concludes on this note: "At Moura, and indeed more generally in the coal industry, there was a quite explicit assumption that it was reasonable to expose miners to danger, provided they voluntarily assumed the risk. From this point of view, the most reprehensible aspect of management behaviour on the night of the explosion was that the men were not given a clear indication that the decision whether to go underground was up to them."[21]

This scenario is about justice, trust, and acceptable safety-related behavior, and what happens when the culture does not value them. It also shows the important role in mindful conduct of widely distributed sensitivity to operations and resilience. Senior management is informed about operations but those on the front line are not. Situational awareness is unevenly distributed. The culture condones these disparities, and there are few mechanisms that encourage people to speak up and inquire about the situation they will face. Norms also preclude candor from management's side. Furthermore, the mine is being run under production pressure, so alternative actions for the dangerous forty-eight-hour explosive period are not drawn up. In other words, the situation is characterized by low resilience, an inadequate repertoire of responses, and low care and concern for key resources.

The phrase *care and concern* comes from crisis researcher Nick Pidgeon's description of what it takes to create a good safety culture: "senior management commitment to safety; shared care and concern for hazards and a solicitude over their impacts on people; realistic and flexible norms and rules about hazards; and continual reflection upon practice through monitoring, analysis, and feedback systems."[22] This is a reasonable description of a mindful culture as well as a safety culture. This parallel again illustrates the point made earlier that strategy can be defined not just by goals to be attained, but also by mistakes to be avoided and mechanisms to avoid them. A mindful culture is saturated with just such mechanisms of error reduction.

Flexible Culture

A *flexible culture* is one that adapts to changing demands. James Reason equates flexibility with the shifting authority structures that we discussed as the fifth process of mindfulness, *deference to expertise*.[23] Our joint focus on this process takes seriously the finding that HROs allow decisions to migrate to expertise during periods of high-tempo activity. The key assumption behind the call for a flexible culture is that information tends to flow more freely when hierarchies are flattened and rank defers to technical expertise. Hence, flexibility and decentralization go hand in hand.

The Moura mine disaster is instructive because it shows a simple but subtle way in which culture can produce a loss of flexibility. The culprit involves what people assume as their default position. In the judgment of Andrew Hopkins, the tragedy at the Moura mine was that people denied that the context was changing and that any flexible response was necessary. They were supported in these denials by a key cultural assumption that was exactly the opposite of the assumption made in most mindful HROs.

People in HROs are able to stay on top of the unexpected because they collect multiple signals from a variety of sources and assemble these signals to see where something does not fit into a pattern. If they find any nonfitting piece, they treat it as a small clue that may point to an enlarging problem. People in

HROs assume that *the system is endangered until there is conclusive proof that it is not.* Any small symptom that doesn't feel right is a clue that safety has not been proven conclusively. If an air traffic controller takes control of a stretch of sky where slow-moving, propeller-driven aircraft are mixed with faster-moving jet aircraft for landing, this mix is an early warning signal that spacing between aircraft could deteriorate rapidly and result in a midair collision. The question is, Does this deviant symptom mean that the system is safe or that the system is in danger? In an HRO, when one symptom is out of line this means that the system is not conclusively safe and may be in danger.

Now, reverse that picture and you can sense what is so worrisome about the cultural assumptions at Moura. At the Moura mine, if one symptom is out of line this means that the system is not conclusively endangered and is safe. A symptom that is out of line is interpreted to mean that the evidence is not conclusive. But nonconclusive relative to what? When data are inconclusive in an HRO, people default to the conclusion that they remain in danger. When data were inconclusive at Moura, people defaulted to the conclusion that they were safe. Whenever multiple symptoms are gathered from diverse sources there is a greater likelihood that some of those symptoms won't fit. This being the case, it matters a great deal what the default position is.

The Moura disaster becomes even more instructive if we probe more deeply into what happens when data are inconclusive. If you assume that inconclusive evidence means that you are safe, you won't dig for more information. If you assume that inconclusive evidence means that you are unsafe, you will dig further. This dynamic contributed to the trouble at the Moura mine. The problem at Moura was that the isolated nature of the symptom was interpreted as proof that the warning was insignificant, not as proof that the context that generated it was poorly understood. Hopkins makes this point forcefully: "If the significance of a warning sign depends on the context then the appropriate response is to investigate the context thoroughly. If a smell is reported, the obvious contextual question to ask is: how many other reports of smells have there been? This question was never asked. To argue that the significance of an indicator depended on the context, but to make no systematic effort to establish the context, nullified the effect of the warning. . . . [At Moura evidence of danger was dismissed as] either irrelevant, to be expected, inconclusive, unsubstantiated, out of context, erroneous or inappropriate."[24]

Learning Culture

If timely, candid information generated by knowledgeable people is available and disseminated, an informed culture becomes a *learning culture.* The combination of candid reporting, justice, and flexibility enable people to witness best practices that occur within their own boundaries and to move toward adoption of them. An informed culture learns by means of ongoing debates about constantly shifting discrepancies. These debates promote learning because they identify new sources of hazard and danger and new ways to cope.

It was hard for people at Moura to learn, partly because anomalies were denied and partly because inquiry, doubt, and updating were discouraged. When anomalies could not be confirmed by one flawed data source, the search stopped and the debate never got off the ground. People did not seek out other sources of data. Instead, they treated the failure to confirm the warnings of benzene as proof that nothing was happening. The benzene was left to accumulate; the unexpected was left to incubate. Furthermore, those who had warned of a potential benzene problem soon learned that mindful action was out of order. If warnings are reasoned away rather than pursued, why bother to voice suspicions in the first place? Nothing will be done anyway. This is the beginning of a deadly drift toward learned helplessness. People learn that escape from bad situations is not under their control, so there is little incentive to respond or to do anything active.[25] Over time, as people grow less and less willing to speak up, this decreases the breadth of observation. As breadth decreases, the number of problems that develop unnoticed increases. The system thus becomes more vulnerable during the very period that it draws precisely the opposite conclusion. It *feels* less vulnerable because there are fewer reports of anomalous events. Learning is stifled because too few data are admitted to prod it.

But learning is also stifled because the assumptions already in place seem innocent enough that there is no need for further inquiry. The Moura mine exploded because people did natural things. People were skeptical about reports so they went to see for themselves what all the fuss was about. They wanted to be safe so they looked for evidence that they were. They wanted to be in control so they neutralized information suggesting that they weren't. People had production quotas to fill so they worked hard to fill them. People reported things that didn't feel right and when others said there was nothing to worry about, they stopped worrying. Culture shapes actions largely without people being aware of how little they see and how many options they overlook. When people are drawn into a culture that is partly of their own making, it is very hard for them to see that what they take for granted hides the beginnings of trouble.

■ Tools to Craft a Mindful Culture

Unexpected events are not simply free-floating hassles that sweep in unannounced and interrupt productive work. Instead, unexpected events are typically authored by the firm itself. Once a firm begins to specify what it expects, it also begins to define what will qualify as an unexpected event. As expectations become clearer, it also becomes clearer what evidence would be inconsistent with them. As we have demonstrated, managing the unexpected means being attentive to both the expected and the unexpected. It also means being attentive to events that lie outside these constructs. If that description begins to sound like the counsel, "Notice everything," that's close. It's an ideal that HROs keep in mind and move toward. Their attentiveness occurs with more or less intensity over a broader or narrower range of issues as a function of how central mindfulness is within the culture. Whether mindfulness is central or not is dependent on how the firm explains the reasons for its successes and failures in coping with problems. If successful coping is attributed to continuous inquiry, candor, wariness, updating, tolerance of discomfort, and flexibility, assumptions supporting mindfulness will be institutionalized in the culture. But if those same successes are attributed instead to factors such as central direction, specialization, confidence, compliance, and confirmed expectations, existing schemes of categorization will be maintained and contexts will be treated as though they are understood even though they are given only cursory attention.

When you think about mindful culture as a means to manage the unexpected, keep the following picture of culture in front of you. Culture is about the assumptions that influence the people who manage the unexpected. Culture can hold large systems together. Culture is unspoken, implicit, taken for granted. You *feel* culture when what you do feels appropriate or inappropriate. You *feel* the unexpected when something surprises you. Culture produces simultaneous centralization-decentralization by binding people to a small set of core values and allowing them discretion over everything else. Culture creates its own discomfort (disconfirmation), its own blind spots, and its own tolerance or intolerance for discomfort and admitting to blind spots. Culture encourages organizationally generated mistakes and it also can discourage them.

To put these ideas in motion, there are several things you can do to influence culture. Although you can't single-handedly change a culture, you can, by the questions you ask and the things you do, move it in the direction of greater mindfulness. Here are some examples of leverage points to do that.

1. *Track down bad news.* Much of the discussion of safety culture boils down to the question, What happens to bad news and to the people who bear it? Ask that question. Don't settle for glib answers. Get others to ask that question.
2. *Clarify the onus of proof.* Ask people whether the current onus of proof operates in the best interests of managing the unexpected. Is the system assumed to be safe until proven dangerous, or dangerous until proven safe? Who decides that? What standard do they use? How many indicators have to line up before people think they really do face something unexpected?
3. *Stalk the anomalous.* Keep asking people, Have you noticed anything out of the ordinary? Praise them for an affirmative answer. And disseminate what they have spotted. What are people *not* seeing? Look for the inconceivable because, in doing so, you are trying to look outside the confines of your current expectations. Deny nothing. Try to see what your expectations keep you from seeing. It's easier to do this when you work with other people and alert them that this is precisely what you're trying to do.
4. *Define the near miss.* Do you know what a near miss is in your organization, and do you talk about near misses when they occur? Do you interpret a near miss as a sign that your system's safeguards are working, or as a sign that the system is

vulnerable? Put discussion of near misses and what they mean higher on your agenda. Raise the comfort level to talk about them.

5. *Consolidate your explanations.* Stop doing anything that interferes with efforts to grasp and describe the context. Things that are out of place in a context bear closer inspection. But be careful of the human tendency to adopt a different explanation for each small deviation. Separate tiny explanations may hide the existence of one big problem. Gary Klein calls this kind of error "de minimus error." People commit this error when they find separate reasons not to take seriously each separate piece of evidence. What they fail to see is that there is one unexpected event that explains them all.

   This type of error is common in medical treatment.[26] A nurse in a neonatal intensive care unit notices that a baby has a distended stomach, blood in the stool, and 3 cc of vomit. She explains away the stomach because his sister had the same condition. She explains away the blood as caused by the nasogastral tube. She explains away the vomit as nothing unusual. The nurse does nothing. The next day the baby is critically ill with an infected bowel. All the symptoms point to this single disorder, but they are never combined, since each one is explained away before the next one is noticed. The person never asks the question, Is there a single diagnosis that fits all these symptoms? Furthermore, if key pieces of information get explained away early, they are no longer available to fill out a pattern that begins to form late in the search. If you explain away the stomach and the blood, you're left late in the examination with vomit that by itself could mean lots of things or nothing at all. Mindfulness keeps track of symptoms, diagnoses, and most important, alternative explanations.

6. *Don't underestimate the power of social influence.* It is not individual attitudes that make it easier or harder to deal with the

unexpected. Instead, the whole reason to be concerned about cultures of mindfulness is that *shared* beliefs, whatever their content, dominate systems. They dominate because they gain their strength from mutual reinforcement. Norms and social control matter.

7. *Examine how your culture treats feedback.* Most descriptions of mindful cultures assume that people have accurate, timely, trusted information about what they are doing and why things go wrong. Often, the value of feedback and perceptions of its importance are affected by whether or not it has any effects. If your culture is drifting toward indifferent feedback practices, take what feedback there is, act on it, and let people see that the action could be better if they were less indifferent about feedback.

8. *Act your way into new values.* If people take actions that are public, irrevocable, and chosen, they tend to be held responsible for those acts by themselves and others. Once they are held responsible for the acts, observers then expect that the people who did those acts must have done them for good reasons. Observers press the actors for their reasons. Likewise, the actors press themselves for their reasons. If the reasons are socially acceptable, save face, and reassure the observers that the actor is a reasonable, rational person, then the reasons are likely to persist and guide future choices. Thus are values born and changed. When it becomes hard to disown an action, it is often easier to alter the values and assumptions that are seen to support it. It is this sense in which culture is something an organization has, and something that it can change.

9. *Don't ignore the "heart" of culture.* As important as it is to think about thinking, the mind, mindfulness, perception, beliefs, expectations, inquiry, and scrutiny, don't forget about *feelings.* They are the engine of culture. Culture consists of expectations (thinking) energized by strong feelings of approval and

disapproval. When people do something that is inappropriate (that is, countercultural) you probably feel yourself wince, get angry, feel embarrassed. You may not even have realized that the action was inappropriate until that feeling welled up. But that's what norms feel like. And that's why they work to control actions far away from corporate headquarters. Culture is about values that matter, approval, disapproval, pride, despair, happiness, hypocrisy, shame, failure. That is strong stuff. Culture pumps feeling and intensity into normally cool ideas, values, and expectations.

10. *Encourage people to paraphrase the key ideas of culture.* Cultures often languish and fail to animate people because they are propped up by mindless repetition of banal phrases. To avoid this, remember that culture takes hold when people express the key ideas in their own words and implement the appropriate behavior in their own way. When US Air changed its name to US Airways, it changed its logo to a stylized gray flag meant to suggest the U.S. flag. But wisely, management never specified precisely what the flag meant or why it was chosen as a logo. Listen to the result: "When asked what the new logo meant, several employees gave interesting answers. 'It's a flag to rally people to take us into battle,' said one pilot. 'It's the one color to show that all the previous mergers have produced this one, united airline,' he added. 'It's supposed to be subdued. It represents our company in transition. When we finish evolving, perhaps it will change,' said yet another. Despite the variety of answers, everyone who was asked had an opinion, a good indication that people in the company are beginning to internalize the changes."[27]

11. *Crystallize the culture in symbols.* Symbols may seem corny, but don't slight them. They can be memorable reminders of what a culture stands for. Gordon Bethune, the imaginative CEO who drafted the turnaround of Continental Air-

lines, is a master of symbols. One of his early innovations was to promise all employees (all forty thousand) a bonus of $65 to be paid at the end of each month that Continental's on-time record placed it among the top five airlines nationwide according to the Department of Transportation's numbers.[28] Continental was dead last in on-time performance when the program was announced in January 1995. In February 1995 they were in fourth place and the checks went out. In March they were in first place for the first time in their history.

That is a story in itself. But the story we're interested in unfolded during a stop on the "road show" that saw Bethune visiting various field stations to explain his priorities. At a meeting in Newark, where he was extolling the bonuses, one employee stood up and said he could certainly understand how people such as gate agents, schedulers, mechanics, baggage handlers, and flight crews would get the bonus. But he couldn't understand why people such as reservation agents who merely answered phones and never laid a hand on a plane "should be getting a share of the dough." How was Bethune going to justify giving away money to people who never got near an airplane as part of their job? Bethune reached up his jacket sleeve, pulled off his watch, held it up, and asked the employee, "Which part of this watch don't you think we need?" The employee had no answer, sat down, and the value of teamwork had just been made palpable. The image of a watch said more about teamwork, more vividly, than any laminated card with the word *Teamwork* splashed on it. Later Bethune drew the moral of the watch more explicitly: "Every part of the watch is not only necessary but as important as every other part. Everybody thinks he or she is the hour hand—everybody thinks he or she is the most important part of the watch. That's just human nature. But for the watch to run, all the parts have to be working. And when you're dealing with human parts, the best way to keep all the parts running is to treat them well."[29]

12. *Exercise control through culture.* Internalized values provide all the centralization you need. A strong culture, held together by consistent values and enforced by social pressure, is all the control you need. Most managers overdo control. They heap hierarchy on top of rules on top of routines on top of job descriptions on top of culture and then wonder why people put forth less than their best. Consensus plus intensity focused on a handful of values is a powerful guide. And sufficient.

Getting the right values is a tough choice. And since you can emphasize only three or four values at most before intensity starts to get diluted and consensus starts to break down, there is not a lot of room for error. AES, a firm we mentioned earlier, is held together by a culture built of four core values (fairness, integrity, social responsibility, fun). Employees who become tightly coupled to these values are given autonomy because they will do the *right thing.* These values matter, as the SEC made clear in a forewarning to investors: "If the company perceives a conflict between its values and profits, the company will try to adhere to its values even if it means a diminishment of profits or foregone opportunities." Chairman Roger Sant underscored the SEC observation when he said, to a *Washington Post* reporter, "Our culture is more important to us than earnings per share." The reason it is more important should be clear. The AES culture is the one thing that enables the firm to disperse decision making throughout the company to people who are closer to the action. Top management still gives advice. But they make very few decisions. The culture guides the rest of the people toward good judgment and good decisions.

13. *Think safety first!* By now you may feel like you're wandering around heavy machinery and everywhere you look you see some sign telling you to be careful. That's just not your circumstance, is it? But think again. Every strategy can be restated as mistakes to be avoided, threats to sidestep, bullets to dodge. Continental Airlines' strategy is to "fund the future," which can be restated as a mistake to avoid, namely, *don't run out of cash.* Similarly, "teamwork matters" means don't play favorites. "Act responsibly" means don't fudge test results to the Environmental Protection Agency. "Be informed" means don't let the ship run aground on your watch. Every strategy has a dark side. And a mindful, reliable safety culture alerts people to the onset of dark moments at earlier stages, when a more decisive remedy is possible.

But "safety first" covers even more than strategy. To be mindful is to dwell on failure, discover the limits of one's control, and uncover more shortcomings than expected. Hence, to be mindful is to be anxious as well. When you're mindful you may question your own competence and mastery. Sure there is challenge and opportunity and stimulation in the discovery that things are not as they seem and that there is much to learn. But you may not be up to doing the necessary learning. Think of the fears felt by people who want to do something about their computer illiteracy but are scared silly that they'll look stupid while doing so. For some, that's too great a price to pay. They'll take illiteracy over looking stupid any day. The point? To be mindful is to become susceptible to learning anxiety. And anxious people need what Edgar Schein calls "psychological safety."[30] People who are made anxious by the prospect of learning need training, support, practice fields, positive role models, and a positive vision that they will be better off with the culture change. Give them that safety. And don't cave in to some kind of silly bravado that says the way we do things around here is to "gut it out," "sink or swim," or "dive off the burning platform." Big deal. If people had been mindful in the first place, they wouldn't need such last-ditch heroics. Moves toward mindfulness are tough. Don't refrain from helping people who are trying to make those moves. And don't be scared to ask for help yourself.

14. *Treat culture as an investment in resilience.* Culture is more aligned with resilience than it is with anticipation. Think about it. Culture gives you a direction, a set of guidelines, and it suggests what to do, *even when events begin to worsen.* Culture doesn't stop giving guidance the minute the situation begins to unravel. Just the opposite. Culture provides an immediate, familiar outline of what you should pay attention to and the constraints within which you should steer your actions. Suppose customer returns of tires or sport utility vehicles or children's high chairs are above normal. Now what? Be fair. Restore reliability. Provide care and concern. Honor your commitments. Do the right thing. Be honest. The recipe for resilience has already been written in the culture. Sure there is a tactical side to "crisis management" that is more detailed than culture guidelines. But those tactics can be derived from the guidelines if the culture has been assembled mindfully, to encourage mindfulness.

15. *Arm yourself for guerilla warfare.* Mindfulness requires continuous, ongoing activity. We are not talking about a "safety war" that ends in victory. We are talking instead about an endless guerilla conflict. Mindful organizations "do not seek a decisive victory, merely a workable survival that will allow them to achieve their productive goals for as long as possible. They know that hazards will not go away. . . .[And they know that they have no choice but to] accept setbacks and nasty surprises as inevitable."[31]

CHAPTER SUMMARY

The message of this chapter is that mindfulness must be treated as a culture as well as a set of processes. If you want to sustain mindful management of the unexpected, you need to embed processes of mindfulness in an integrated set of values, expectations, and norms that encourage appropriate attitudes and behaviors and discourage inappropriate ones. That *integrated set* is what people have in mind when they talk about corporate culture. Culture is a pattern of shared beliefs and expectations that shape how individuals and groups act. Culture exerts centralized control over dispersed activities by means of a handful of core values that are credibly enacted by top management, widely accepted by people in the organization, and used with intensity to interpret and express appropriate behaviors.

A mindful culture resembles an informed safety culture. We used this resemblance to show how inattention to mindfulness contributed to the Moura mine disaster and how more reliance on mindful processes might have forestalled the tragedy. Larger lessons learned from the Moura disaster included the need to clarify the default position in assessing danger, the need to look more closely at possible negative consequences of straightforward assumptions, and the importance of remaining attentive to context and any signs that something out of the ordinary is unfolding. Moving away from the Moura disaster and safety culture, we ended with a summary of several tools that can make the organization's habits of thought more visible and point the way to habits that foster a more mindful culture.

How to Manage Mindfully

indfulness is as much a mindset as it is a style of managing. Right this minute, you probably know more about that mindset than anyone else in your firm. You've immersed yourself in examples and descriptions of mindfulness that bring alive just what it is and what it accomplishes. You have some idea of how to spot more and less mindful moments in your firm and culture. And you have some ideas about how to shift your culture toward a greater emphasis on mindfulness. But culture change takes a long time. And it is susceptible to influence from many more directions than simply your own intentions.

So that leaves your own style of managing as the most immediate, the most influential, and the most controllable means to start managing the unexpected. If you convert a mindfulness mindset into a mindful style of managing, you don't have to wait for slow culture change to take hold. Instead, you can manage differently the moment you lay down this book. Nothing could be more immediate. Managing with a more mindful style can also be more influential because people can see firsthand, in your actions, that mindfulness is practical, doable, and makes a difference. That is a powerful lesson. It will encourage others to follow your lead and adopt some of the tools you use to stay on top of the unexpected. And these immediate, influential changes in your style of managing are something that you control. If you want to act with more mindfulness, it's within your power to do so. Mindful management for assured high performance starts with you. You know how it works. You know why it works. You know where it works. And now you can make it work where it matters most, in the world that controls your fate.

This last chapter is an effort to coach and support your moves toward a more mindful style. We begin the chapter by returning to where we started, with the Union Pacific Railroad in deep trouble and close to gridlock. Since those dark days, the UP's performance suggests that in some ways they still don't get it and other ways they do. The "it" that they sometimes get and sometimes don't is the necessity to act with more mindfulness to better assure reliable performance in the face of unexpected events. People at the UP still get trapped by some of the same assumptions, beliefs, and behaviors that may keep you from managing with more mindfulness. But the UP has also had some successes. Their stretches of mindless action are now broken up more often with mindful moments. There are clear lessons for you in the ongoing ups and downs at UP: Adopt what works for them and discard everything else, even if people keep telling you that what you're discarding is the "core" of rational management. You know better. After we get some closure on the UP as a firm actively struggling with reliability, high performance, mindfulness, and the unexpected, we conclude the chapter with a review of key points. But the key points now are stated in the form of guidelines for managing. These guidelines convert the mindfulness mindset into prescriptions for action. And these prescriptions are the raw materials from which you can fashion your own distinctive managerial style that is heavy on mindfulness and light on its feet in the face of the unexpected.

■ Failures and Successes of Mindfulness at Union Pacific

We began this book with a group of railroaders who were mindless in Houston. It seems only fair that we revisit these people to see how the Union Pacific–Southern Pacific merger is going. Some of the recent public statements suggest that the merger is going well and that the Union Pacific is more mindful and more profitable. But other statements suggest otherwise. You be the judge.

Mindfulness Failures at UP

Since the meltdown at the Englewood yard, the eleven fatalities, the enraged shippers, the $4 billion hit to the U.S. economy, the loss of shipments to trucks, barges, and rail competitors such as the Burlington Northern–Santa Fe (BNSF), the lawsuits, and the temporary special constraints imposed by the Surface Transportation board, people at UP have spent $2 billion on capital improvements.[1,2] They've used the money to lay track, buy locomotives, link railyards, hire people, and blend computer systems. In other words, they've used the money to do basically the same things they've been doing all along. Though these actions may look like a preoccupation with failure and greater sensitivity to operations, they largely involve old categories that are applied with neither refinement nor differentiation. Furthermore, the context is being read in the same old ways; new dimensions or distinctions are not being suggested, and new routines are not being enacted. It is business as usual, albeit with a new urgency and in a far more hostile environment.

In some ways these are the easy changes to make. It is easier to buy stuff than it is to create and stabilize new ways of relating one function to another. Relationships, people issues, expectations, norms—those are the tough, messy issues. And as you might expect, culture change at UP is lagging. But then again, it lags everywhere. That is why many of the moves toward mindfulness at UP seem tentative, modest, and potentially transient. Even though there are bits and pieces of mindfulness already evident, the UP does not yet have a culture that binds those pieces together, animates them, institutionalizes them, and makes them prominent, consistent, and credible from top to bottom in the corporation. For example, on the first page of the Letter from the Chairman in the 1998 UP annual report, CEO Davidson said the following about "transforming the culture":

> The railroad franchise is the backbone of our ability to deliver value to customers and ultimately to shareholders. But to achieve the potential of this franchise, we need a culture and an organizational structure that enable our people to do their best. We learned this the hard way during our service difficulties. We wanted to make sure these hard-earned lessons were not forgotten but were put to work to make Union Pacific a stronger company. . . . [W]e began to change the culture of our company, uniting our employees under a common vision and common set of values. While perhaps the most difficult to quantify, we believe this culture change will result in the most positive and far-reaching impact of all.[3]

Admirable as this sounds, UP is not there yet. A recent employee survey gave low marks to management for not realizing that employees' ideas are important, not giving enough feedback, and not recognizing workers' efforts.[4] Listen closely to how Davidson reacted to these survey results. Davidson said that these results show encouraging trends "that meant they're worrying about the right things. And these are problems we can do something about."[5] Did you notice the pronouns? They're worrying, we're doing. We versus they. It sounds as though the famous "bright white line" that divides UP's management from UP's workers is alive and well and undisturbed by adversity. At least at the top.

Mindfulness Successes at UP

From the standpoint of mindfulness, the UP isn't hopelessly stuck. There are snatches of mindfulness in several places. For example, there is a growing sensitivity to operations. This is evident in alterations to the Englewood yard. It is now connected to other yards, which makes it possible for inbound trains to be handled in one yard, an SP yard, and outbound trains in another yard, a UP yard. Flexibility has been restored to operations by means of a new system of directional running. In three states where SP and UP tracks are roughly parallel, the UP track handles all traffic moving in one direction, and the separate SP tracks handle all traffic moving in the opposite direction. As the *Houston Chronicle* reported, this eliminated 41,000 times a year that a train had to pull into a side track and stop so that a train going in the other direction could pass.[6] There are also intricate efforts at joint dispatching with the BNSF to avoid potential bottlenecks in the Texas area.

Structure has become more decentralized. Decision making is now pushed down to key people in three regions rather than centralized in Omaha. Decentralization moves decisions closer to the action and heightens the sensitivity to operations. The moves toward decentralization also counteract the simplifying tendencies of corporate officers in distant Omaha. Corporate tends to treat the 36,000-mile system of major coal fields, inter-modal shipping of containers from Pacific ships, central U.S. grain shipments, and Gulf Coast petrochemical products as though it were one big, rail-dependent, homogenous shipper. De-centralization helps differentiate that picture. Finally, decentral-ization may be a sign of more deference to expertise, as well as a grudging admission from the top that others with less authority but more experience may know something worth knowing.

One of the most interesting moves toward mindfulness is a new Network Design and Integration (NDI) group.[7] The purpose of this group is to match capability and assets with business de-mands. There is a concerted effort to realize that the railroad can-not be all things to all people. In the words of NDI, "Do we want to handle all commodities on all segments? No." To implement this purpose there are separate asset teams that focus on corridor performance, locomotives, freight cars, engineering, commercial facilities, information technology, communications, and man-power. Their assessments feed into a six-person lead team that includes the executive vice president of operations, and the ex-ecutive vice presidents for marketing, finance, information tech-nology, and strategic planning.

If you put on your management hat you say to yourself, Ho-hum, here is one more effort to break out of functional silos. But if you put on your mindfulness hat, you see something a lit-tle different. You see that silos are a form of simplification and the teams are an effort to resist simplification. The asset teams at UP represent an effort to think in new categories of *capability* and *demand,* not the old categories of marketing, finance, oper-ations. The teams represent an effort to take a simple context—any old warm body is a potential customer—and differentiate those warm bodies into customers they can handle, customers they can't handle, customers they don't want to handle. There is a conscious effort to direct a more diverse set of perspectives at what is viewed as a more complicated problem. When you think in terms of mindfulness you see, in the asset groups, a tangible example of requisite variety. You see an attempt on the part of UP to match the variety in a complex environment of commodity customers with an equally complex set of sensors that can read that complexity. If early signs suggest that demands are moving in unexpected directions, people can redeploy railroad assets to meet those changes. These are the same kinds of diverse groups that kept Diablo Canyon safe. These are the same kinds of groups that force any organization to question itself, look for evidence that disconfirms its cherished expectations, and see beyond its simplifications.

Perhaps most important, it is the asset group taken together—not necessarily any one individual in the group—that can maintain the bubble of current operations. Because of their constant interactions, any one member of the group knows how the other members see things, which means any one individual has a bigger picture than before. That is a huge advantage when coordinated performance is crucial. But even more important is the fact that the asset group *jointly* maintains the bubble and has keen situational awareness of what is happening. Even though this understanding in one sense is distributed among several people, in another sense that understanding is consolidated and takes the form of coordinated, complementary efforts that make for a *system* that is smarter than any one person in it.[8] It is that accomplishment that provides a competitive advantage that is tough to imitate.

Some of the energy for rethinking the UP has come from its new president and COO, Ike Evans. He joined UP as an outsider, having come from a senior vice presidency at Emerson Electric. He brings fresh eyes and a different set of simplifications to the railroad. He saw the meltdown in operations as an outsider, not as an insider who had to put the best face on a railroad in disarray. Evans saw more clearly the liabilities of arrogance than did those on the inside. And he may have learned the lessons of

UP's failure more clearly. Insiders whose egos and reputations were on the line couldn't afford to look the failure square in the eye for fear of what it would say about them. Consequently, the "hard-earned lessons" that Davidson mentioned in the Annual Report may have been closer to softballs than hardballs. Yes, some things were learned. But they were changes at the margins. Evans didn't have as much invested in the failures, so he could afford to study them more closely. And with his efforts come some interesting twists for mindfulness.

Under Evans, for example, the railroad is reinvigorating its quality program. Davidson refers to this in the Annual Report as "re-energizing quality." The prefix "re" shows up repeatedly in references to this program, as in reenergizing, reemphasis on quality process, reinvigorating quality. So what? So, again in Davidson's words, "Quality has been a driving force at UP since 1987, but with the distractions of the mergers and the difficulties of the service crisis, we lost our quality discipline."[9] The *so what* in all of this is that the UP is reaching back to the discredited Mike Walsh era and trying to reactivate the culture changes that Walsh designed and set in motion. Walsh, the outsider, saw needs that Davidson the insider didn't see. And Walsh the outsider started the quality emphasis. The insiders did not embrace it. Walsh moved on, quality languished, UP got expansive, it disregarded the unexpected strains that were building up, and serious harm resulted. There are lessons here for outsider Evans. And for insider Davidson.

Organizing for Mindfulness at UP

All these successes and failures are affected by how the organization itself functions. We're not talking here about organizations viewed as rational, goal-driven, hierarchical designs with specialized tasks that, when assembled, implement what strategists and planners set in motion. Actually, we don't see many organizations that look like this. And neither do you. What you and Ike Evans and Dick Davidson see more of are social organizations. These are places where people and their tendencies give a distinctive form to the proceedings. These are places where "information is limited and serves largely to justify decisions or positions already taken; goals, preferences and effectiveness criteria are problematic and conflicting; organizations are loosely linked to their social environments; the rationality of various designs and decisions is inferred after the fact to make sense out of things that have already happened; organizations are coalitions of various interests; organization designs are frequently unplanned and are basically responses to contests among interests for control over the organization; and organization designs are in part ceremonial."[10] That description rings true because it is about people and how they behave and interact. That's what you and the UP have to work with in your efforts to head off unexpected threats to high performance, earlier, through mindful action.

Notice that when we take the social side of organizations seriously, we can see more clearly why it is so tough to move toward mindfulness. Social organizations tend to gather information selectively to justify decisions. But if you want to manage the unexpected with mindfulness, you need detailed information that disconfirms as well as justifies. Mindfulness also involves preferences that are diverse; close attention to situations; resilience in the face of events; sensemaking that shows whether a decision is necessary; people with diverse interests who debate, speak up, and listen to one another; and designs that are malleable rather than fixed. Many of these changes are at odds with the directions of a social organization. This means that when you try to move people toward mindfulness, you often move them in unfamiliar directions. They may resist. Why? Partly because of threats to psychological safety. Maybe I'm not up to acting more mindfully. Maybe I'll look stupid. Maybe I *am* stupid. After all, it's a whole lot easier to bask in success, keep it simple, follow routines, avoid trouble, and do an adequate job. I know how to do those things. But dwell on failure? Question my assumptions? Linger over details? Fight fires creatively? Ask for help? No thanks. Or more likely, "You first!"

■ Managing for Mindfulness at Your Firm

You first! That's the challenge for UP. It's the challenge for you. Someone has to wade in, show the way, show what mindfulness looks like, and show how higher performance is assured if unexpected threats are detected earlier and contained more efficiently.

So what's your judgment about the UP? Do you see a move in the general direction of greater mindfulness? Or do you see the same old mindlessness with the same old occasional pockets of mindfulness? Or do you see perhaps a balance of mindful-mindless action? Now ask those same questions about yourself and your group.

The moment you put this book down, you can start taking action. We urge you to do so. We urge the top management team at UP, the Moura mine managers, the AES entrepreneurs, the Diablo Canyon operators, the Continental Airlines reservation agents, the R & D people at Coca-Cola Company, the air bosses on carriers, the overworked nurses in intensive care units, and the crew chiefs of wildland firefighting crews, all to wade in and pay closer attention to what is going on right now. But more important, we urge that you carry your labels for what is going on right now *lightly*. Be prepared to replace them with labels and verbs that pry loose some qualities of your situation that most everyone else missed. That's challenging. That's diagnosis. That's detective work. That's fun. That's mindfulness. Here's how you get there.

Effective high reliability organizations are made up of people like you who have developed ways to work in fluid but orderly ways to focus energy and expertise where and when they are needed. Their secret, one you can adopt, is that they have developed mindful styles of behaving that both encourage continuous learning and promote order and reliable performance in the face of the unexpected. This is a powerful combination, one that most organizations would be happy to achieve. You can be an important champion and role model to show that this ideal can be approximated in your firm. Concrete ways for you to do this are suggested by the mindfulness maxims presented in this section. These maxims summarize key lessons learned from HROs. These lessons are restated in ways that are designed to help you strengthen your capabilities to cope more effectively with the unexpected. Although many practices are relevant, we focus on those that show up repeatedly in the best HROs and directly relate to the five processes that create a mindful infrastructure. As we did in Chapter Three, we organize these processes under the headings of (1) awareness and anticipation of the unexpected and (2) containment of those unexpected events that occur.

Enhancing Awareness and Anticipation

In this book we have focused on the interval between anticipation and resilience during which the unexpected is detected more or less swiftly and managed more or less successfully. Members of organizations that sense problems earlier seem to maintain high self-consciousness about beliefs and their validity, institutional support for ongoing doubt, updating, and learning, attention to here and now activity, and active contesting of interpretations. The following suggestions can enhance your ability to spot unforeseen events more quickly.

- Preserve a balance of values. There are many approaches to building a corporate culture that values both production and protection, but all require the active involvement of company leaders. The values and expectations that leaders communicate through their actions (where they focus their attention, how they react to unexpected events, to whom they allocate rewards, and decisions about whom to recruit or dismiss) send important messages to organizational members about the kinds of behaviors that are desired. To remain competitive in an increasingly dynamic environment, leaders will have to help employees learn to cope with the tension of conflicting aims rather than choosing one goal over the other.

- Restate your goals in the form of mistakes that must not occur. Doing so will focus more attention directly on the unexpected, on disconfirmed expectations, and on issues of reliability.

- Remember that mindfulness takes effort. Mindfulness is difficult to create because you're asking people to act unnaturally. In the interest of more mindfulness, you're asking people to pay more attention to their failures than to their successes, forgo recipes and rules of thumb in favor of what amounts to reinventing the wheel every time they act, pay attention to tactics and nuts and bolts rather than strategies and grand visions, get better at being reactive rather than proactive, and acknowledge that someone else may know more than they do. That's a big order. People would prefer to pay more attention to success, recipes, strategies, initiatives, and status. As an intermediate step in moving toward greater mindfulness, try to increase the number of mindful moments in your unit. A mindful moment consists of a short interval, such as trying to solve a modest problem, where people agree to look at failures, assume nothing, look closely at the work involved in the problem, brainstorm a resilient response, and pinpoint the expert in handling the problem rather than the person accountable for the problem.

■ Create awareness of vulnerability. Get comfortable asking people, What's risky around here? Managers must sensitize employees to the possibility of unexpected errors that could escalate. People need to worry about vulnerability and feel accountable for reliability. Awareness of vulnerability increases opportunities for learning and is central to reliable, failure-free performance. This awareness is evident in two ways: first, in people's commitment to reliability, and second, in their recognition that even though they think they understand their system and the ways in which it can fail, surprises are still possible. They have neither seen every possible failure mode in their everyday life nor imagined every possible one. Complacence is inappropriate.

■ Cultivate humility. Appreciate the traps inherent in short-term success and false optimism. Success narrows perceptions, changes attitudes, feeds confidence in a single way of doing business, breeds overconfidence in the efficacy of current abilities and practices, and makes people less tolerant of opposing points of view. Try to see the value of increasing organizational learning through a healthy skepticism about your own accomplishments and a greater awareness of potential for failure.

■ Be glad when you're having a bad day! When things go wrong, you uncover more details and learn more about how things work. Pessimism is more mindful than is optimism. The tricky part is to keep going in the face of bad news. The bad news of mistakes, recast as the good news of enlarged learning and deeper understanding, can nudge motivation higher.

■ Create an error-friendly learning culture. Work-group learning requires a number of behaviors that include seeking feedback, sharing information, asking for help, talking about errors, and experimenting. It is through these activities that groups can detect changes in the environment, learn about customers' requirements, improve members' collective understanding of a situation, or discover unexpected consequences of previous actions. Yet learning is curtailed in many organizational contexts when people in positions to initiate learning perceive they are placing themselves at risk in terms of their career or their image if they admit an error, ask for help, or seek feedback. Through your actions and expectations, create a climate of openness in which people feel safe to surface unexpected events rather than covering them up, ask for help if they need it, and seek feedback. Make it easy for people to confess errors.

- Encourage alternative frames of reference. Reward units, teams, and groups that preserve divergent analytical perspectives. Divergent perspectives provide you with a broader set of assumptions and sensitivity to a greater variety of inputs. This discourages simplification and also increases the chance of seeing a greater number of problems in the making. Practices that encourage divergence in analytical perspectives include a proliferation of committee meetings, frequent adversarial reviews, selecting new employees with nontypical prior experience, frequent job rotation, and retraining.

- Strengthen fantasy as a tool for managing the unexpected. Mindful management of the unexpected consists of numerous moments of extrapolation of possible effects of small discrepancies, imagination of scenarios not yet experienced, mental simulation of the consequences of interactions among simultaneously occurring weak anomalies, hypothetical construction of alternative lines of action, and envisioning of what might have been overlooked given the narrow focus of a set of well-supported expectations. These are operations of fantasy that can feel alien in cultures obsessed with measurement and quantification. For example, you can devote time in management and executive meetings to simulating alternative scenarios of anticipated futures, and working backward from an imagined outcome to identify the events that could bring that outcome about. Alternatively you can give individuals or groups assignments to imagine scenarios and write them up.

- Speak up! Just because you see something, don't assume that someone else sees it, too. In a world of multiple realities and multiple expectations, one person's signal is another person's noise. Don't voluntarily withdraw dissent. When you do so, you reduce the system's ability to detect the unexpected.

- Put a premium on interpersonal skills. Variety has a price. The price is that it can increase the incidence of disagreement and conflict when it comes time to act. Strengthen skills of conflict resolution and negotiation. Foster norms of mutual respect for differences—norms that curb bullheadedness, hubris, headstrong acts, and self-importance. Develop organizational agreements about how to disagree agreeably, propose rules for negotiating differences, and develop policies that reconcile organizational contradictions (for example, rewarding individuals while supporting the value of collaboration and cooperation).

- Surface unique knowledge. The useful outcomes of variety sometimes go unrealized. Members of groups tend not to share the unique knowledge they hold and prefer instead to talk most about information they all hold in common. Rely on process mechanisms such as brainstorming or the nominal group technique that encourage people to raise questions and reveal information that is not widely shared.[11] Acknowledge the presence of competition for resources and how politics and turf wars can inhibit free information exchange.

- Be careful when you label something a fact. Once you call something a fact you pay less attention to it. If you pay less attention, there will be less chance that you will see exceptions that call into question its facticity. There are two problems here. First, you are likely to attribute more stability to events than is warranted. Second, you may unwittingly treat your behavior of not monitoring as evidence of factualness. In either case, you overestimate the stability of an event and may miss its continuing contribution to the unexpected.

▪ Develop skeptics. Skepticism is an odd form of redundancy. When a report is met with skepticism and the skeptic makes an independent effort to confirm the report, there are now two observations where there was originally one. The second set of observations may support or refute the first set and may itself be double-checked by still another skeptic. Skepticism thus counteracts complacency and provides a more nuanced description of the context that in turn may suggest more ways to deal with it.

▪ Be suspicious of good news. There is always bad news, and if you get none, someone is hiding something.

▪ Seek out bad news. Research suggests that subordinates are more likely to report good news to their superiors than bad. This pattern is strengthened when those in power dismiss bad news that threatens their prevailing worldviews. Sometimes people in high places dismiss news because they overestimate the likelihood that they would surely know about a situation if it actually were taking place. To counter this tendency, seek out bad news or news that is contrary to prevailing views. One of the best ways to encourage subordinates to report bad news is to respond in the following way. When someone brings bad news to your attention say: Really? Tell me more. What do you think we should do about it? Thanks for bringing this to my attention.

▪ Test your expectations. It's easy to overestimate the accuracy and soundness of what are actually flawed expectations. To test your understanding of events, write down your expectations, in advance, of how they will unfold. When the events actually occur, you can then spot shortfalls in your understanding by spotting which expectations didn't pan out. People always think they have a better set of expectations than they do because they keep revising them unwittingly with the benefit of hindsight.

▪ Welcome uncertainty. If you're uncertain, that's a good sign that you're in touch with reality because there is little that is certain in the indeterminate world of trying to organize in the face of continuous change.

▪ Treat all unexpected events as information, and share this information widely. Use unexpected events as data points for learning, especially if they rarely occur. Be especially mindful of the temptation to redefine the unexpected as the expected. That move conceals information and heightens risk. Treat small lapses as weak signals that other portions of the system may be at risk. Suspect that the causal chains that produced the event wind deep inside the system. Communicate this information widely.

▪ Transform close calls into near misses. A near miss is a more vivid free lesson that "vaccinates" people by helping them learn more about their defenses. When you relabel a *close call* as a *near miss*, you make it clearer that the event was evidence of danger in the guise of safety rather than evidence of safety in the guise of danger. Danger disguised as safety is a stronger warning of vulnerability than is safety disguised as danger. A near miss is also a near hit. A close call is also a close what? That's the point. To call something a *near miss* is to say more and to call for more.

▪ Specify the burden of proof. Systems become more vulnerable to costly disruption if they fail to address the question, Where does the burden of proof lie in expectations of safety? Is the system presumed safe unless proved dangerous, or is it presumed dangerous unless proved safe? The presumption of danger tends to heighten awareness more than does the presumption of safety.

▪ Adopt complex models because they direct attention to more details and register more facets of context. Complex models are easier to come by if you resist the temptation to keep it simple.

- Revise existing models as well as existing practices. Classify unexpected events not on the basis of the severity of the consequences that follow them, but on the degree to which they deviate from the prevailing models of what was expected. Update old models and revise practice based on new understandings. By refreshing, renewing, and rejecting procedures, you encapsulate new experience, thereby mitigating complacency and rigidity.

- Carry your expectations lightly. Their disconfirmation will be less painful, their revision will be more likely, and this whole process of learning will be experienced as more pleasurable. But be aware that if expectations are held lightly, they will give less guidance, and this will impose greater demands on attention. Since attention is a scarce resource, make efforts to identify dimensions that are being ignored.

- Reward contact with the front line. Reward managers who stay close to the operating system or the frontline activities. Sensitivity to operations is a powerful means to keep up with developing situations. Managers who demonstrate ongoing attention to operations create a context where surprises are more likely to be surfaced and corrected before they grow into problems.

- Clarify what constitutes good news. Is *no news* good news or is it bad news? Don't let this remain a question. Remember, no news can mean either that things are going well or that someone is incapacitated and unable to give news, which is bad news. Don't fiddle with this one. No news is bad news. All news is good news, because it means that the system is in place and responsive. The good system talks incessantly. When it goes silent, that's unexpected, that's trouble, that's bad news.

- Frame mindfulness in novel ways. AES says and does some strange things, and one of the most unusual is their insistence that they "try to reinvent the wheel every chance we get."[12] Think about it. Reinventing the wheel is supposed to be the last thing any of us would want to do. And yet each time you reinvent the wheel you're a slightly different person from the last time you reinvented the wheel. And those intervening experiences may just enable you to see something in the reinvention that you missed every time before, something that this time will give you an advantage over those whose reinvention is a perfect replica of every other reinvention. Isn't that the essence of mindfulness? To be more mindful is to see things you missed, details that foreshadow new consequences, unsuspected leverage points, unforeseen vulnerabilities, and sequences that can be rearranged. Mindfulness amounts to seeing old things in new ways, which is pretty much the challenge when you try to reinvent the wheel, but with a new understanding of what *wheel* means.

Enhancing Containment

The preceding maxims are suggestions for improving competence in anticipating and becoming aware of unexpected events. The following ideas are designed to build competence to contain or bounce back from inevitable problems once they become evident.

• Remember that ambivalence builds resilience. When the unexpected deteriorates into a serious disruption, this result is an outcome that is partly novel and partly routine. You've seen lots of messes, but you've never seen quite this particular mess. This means that your past experience is both partly relevant and partly irrelevant. Begin to contain the event by doing what experience tells you to do, but remain in doubt that you're doing exactly the right thing. Watch for what you have not seen before and deal with it immediately, but retain the context created by your past experience in the interest of keeping your intervention meaningful. This is less crazy than it sounds. You're simply engaging in simultaneous belief and doubt, admittedly a difficult exercise. Your goal is to act simultaneously as though the unexpected situation you face is just like every other situation you've faced and like no other situation you've ever faced. Maintaining ambivalence will tend to increase information intake as well as the appropriateness of the action, all while you continue to do something familiar that at least stabilizes the situation.

- Use rich media and encourage people to listen.[13] Unexpected events are often confusing and people need to use rich media to build some idea of what they face. Face-to-face communication is generally regarded as the richest medium, and richness declines as people move to interaction by telephone, written personal communiqués (letters and memos), written formal communiqués (bulletins), and numeric formal communiqués (printouts). Face to face is the richest because of the capacity for timely feedback, the ability to convey multiple cues, the degree to which the message can be personalized, the variety of language that can be used, and the range of meaning that can be conveyed. As richness is lost, so is key information. Debates about launching the *Challenger* spacecraft in unusually cold temperatures were conducted over a telephone, not face to face. With only voice cues, NASA did not have visual data such as facial expressions that might have given them fuller information about just how worried Thiokol engineers were at the prospect of a launch. An important caution turns on norms for the appropriate conduct of face-to-face communication. When people discuss confusing events they sometimes think they have to convince others of the validity of their own perspective and fail to listen respectfully and attentively to what others say. When this happens advocacy replaces analysis, both richness and mindfulness are lost, and containment suffers. *Challenger* is launched. Make sure everyone's voice is heard.

- Be mindful publicly. Think out loud when you question categories, propose refinements, spot limitations, and see new features of context. When you inquire publicly this helps people understand what is going on and provides a model for them to imitate. Overt displays of thought are a good thing. Overt displays of mindful thought are an even better thing.

- Enlarge competencies and response repertoires. Resilience takes deep knowledge. Generalized training, both through frequent job rotation and learning from mistakes, is important because it increases people's response repertoires, thus in turn enlarging the range of issues that they notice and can deal with. When people enlarge their capability for action, they can see more hazards because whatever they see, they will have some way to deal with it.

- Build excess capacity. Don't overdo lean, mean ideals. The lean, mean organization may sparkle in the short run, but it may also crash and burn at the first unexpected jolt because leanness strips the organization of resilience and flexibility. Realize that when managers eliminate "redundant" positions, they sacrifice experience and expertise. That loss can limit the repertoire of responses available to the organization. Improve resilience by harnessing knowledgeable people into ad hoc networks that self-organize to provide expert problem solving. These networks are a source of generalized, uncommitted resources that are necessary to cope in a resilient manner with the unexpected.

- Create flexible decision structures. When problems occur, let decision making migrate to people who have the most expertise to deal with the problem. This means that expertise and experience are more highly valued than rank when unexpected situations arise.

- Accelerate feedback. Effective resilience requires quick, accurate feedback so that the initial effects of attempted improvisations can be detected quickly and the action altered or abandoned if the effects are making things worse.[14] Systems with slow feedback essentially give up any chance for resilience. And in an era in which more and more challenges are unexpected and tough to anticipate, any loss in resilience is a serious blow to survival.

- Balance centralization with decentralization. When people have discretion to act on problems, they develop a more elaborate sensing mechanism capable of detecting possible dangers on a local level. This delegated capacity for local detection must be held simultaneously with a centralized capacity that maintains the organization's larger awareness of its vulnerability and serves to coordinate responses and learning that occur at the local level. In HROs decentralization and centralization are held in critical balance, often by means of tight social coupling around a handful of core cultural values and looser coupling around the means by which these values are realized. Excess centralization can weaken local containment and resolution of problems, whereas excess decentralization can weaken the comprehension of wider threats and the capacity to coordinate responses.

- Reinforce perishable values. Resilient containment and reactive responsiveness are made possible by continuous reinforcement of three values: credibility, trust, and attentiveness.

- Mitigate complacency. One of the more vivid "truths" known to HROs is that the past settles its accounts when something unexpected begins to incubate. Crisis expert Pat Lagadec has stated this point quite well: "The ability to deal with a crisis situation is largely dependent on structures that have been developed before chaos arrives. The event can in some ways be considered an abrupt and brutal audit: at a moment's notice, everything that was left unprepared becomes a complex problem, and every weakness comes rushing to the forefront. The breech in the defences opened by crisis creates a sort of vacuum."[15] When the trains began to back up in Texas, earlier failures to integrate functions, become more quality conscious, decentralize, add general resources, and listen rather than tell came home to haunt the UP. The stalled trains audited a system that was deficient in resilience and deference, and those weaknesses "came rushing to the forefront." Competitors, infuriated shippers, regulators, lawyers, and unions swept into the "vacuum" and made resilience even more difficult. Containment is something that can be anticipated, rehearsed, and prepared for by increasing knowledge and capability. Are you ready for a brutal audit of your capability to act mindfully in later stages of unfolding disconfirmations? Is your group ready? They aren't ready if people don't even know the costs of mindless action in a complex, unpredictable world. They aren't ready if they don't know that unexpected events incubate. They aren't ready if they don't know that their own tendencies to prepare for managing the unexpected are likely to be mindless and make the situation worse, rather than to be mindful and make the situation better. And they aren't ready if they don't have deepening knowledge of and experience with their work. Those are tough lessons for people in high places to learn. Best get on with disseminating them.

CHAPTER SUMMARY

In this chapter we have focused on how you can make your own style of management more mindful.

We looked first at specific efforts by the Union Pacific Railroad to deal with disastrous gridlock in their system. We found some changes that could be interpreted as efforts to deal with the unexpected more mindfully. A good example was the creation of a new and diverse group dedicated to integration of the system. What was noteworthy about their efforts was the development of a new set of categories and distinctions for customer demands that allowed for better use of railroad assets. This group looked for failures, dissected assumptions, got closer to operations, and helped push decision making closer to experts—all key processes that enhance mindfulness. The implicit message was that mindfulness might be easier to develop in groups rather than one person at a time. The reason for this is that individuals prefer to dwell on success, keep it simple, follow routines, avoid trouble, and equate expertise with rank. All these preferences run contrary to mindfulness. In a diverse group focused on a specific problem, people tend to become more conscious of these tendencies and to question their value in solving the problem. Although the UP showed some mindful moments, there were indications that the pregridlock culture was intact. The implication was clear for UP, as it is for you, that continuous, long-term efforts are necessary if mindfulness is to be spread around to more people managing more issues, and if unexpected gridlock is to be avoided in the future.

The second half of the chapter described a number of actions that enable you to embed mindful anticipation and mindful resilience in your style of managing. If that embedding occurs, associates who pay close attention to whether you walk your talk will see more clearly how mindfulness works. And they'll also see that you're serious about mindfulness and will begin, themselves, to walk the talk they saw you initiate. The actions that were suggested for incorporation into your management style were quite varied. But they all derive from the same premise: If you update and differentiate the labels you impose on the world, the unexpected will be spotted earlier and dealt with more fully, and sustained high performance will be more assured. Reliability is a dynamic event and gets compromised by distraction and ignorance. Mindfulness is about staying attuned to what is happening and about a deepening grasp of what those events mean.

Mindfulness is not just about issues of safety and crisis. Mindfulness is about the unexpected events that show up everywhere in corporate life, but also in our other lives as well. Whether we like it or not, if the world is filled with the unexpected, we're all firefighters putting out one fire after another. Most people resist that depiction and like to lay claim to loftier activities, greater control, and bolder initiatives. People want to get away from fighting fire so they can get to the good stuff, such as planning, making strategy, crafting vision, forecasting, and anticipating. Those are supposed to be the high-prestige pastimes where one finds the real action. The world of managing the unexpected through mindfulness suggests a different picture of prestigious action. As you implement the practices discussed throughout this book, you'll discover that plans and visions and forecasts are inaccurate and gain much of their power from efforts to avoid disconfirmation. You'll also discover that plans and visions and forecasts create blind spots. Corrections to those inaccuracies lie in the hands of those who have a deeper grasp of how things really work. And that grasp comes from mindfulness. People who act mindfully notice and pursue that rich, neglected remainder of information that mindless actors leave unnoticed and untouched. Mindful people hold complex projects together because they understand what is happening. That is what HROs can teach you.

Notes

Chapter One

1. This sequence adapted from Barry A. Turner and Nick F. Pidgeon, *Man-made Disasters,* 2nd ed. (Oxford, England: Butterworth-Heinemann, 1997), p. 117.
2. Wendy Zellner, "An Old Brakeman Faces His Ultimate Test," *Business Week* (October 6, 1997): 110–115.
3. June 22 at Devine, Texas, two UP freights collided head-on, killing two crew members and two trespassers; July 2 at Kenefick, Kansas, freight train failed to stop at signal and collided with oncoming train, engineer killed; August 20 in Fort Worth, Texas, unattended set of coupled locomotives started moving, accelerated to sixty miles per hour and collided with freight train leaving Centennial Yard, killing engineer and engineer pilot; August 23 at Shawnee Junction, Wyoming, a unit coal train struck the rear of a standing coal train, two injured; August 31 in Barstow, California, freight train struck rear of standing freight, one injured; October 25 in Houston two freights collided head-on, four injured. These data were compiled by Catherine Augustine.
4. Jack Burke, "UP Unravels Further," *Traffic World* (September 1, 1997): 22–23; see p. 22.
5. Fred W. Frailey, "Union Pacific's Texas Traffic Jam," *Trains* (January, 1998): 26.

6. Allen R. Myerson, "Hearings Focus on Union Pacific Rail Safety," *New York Times* (March 18, 1998).

7. Freight trains were parked in sidings when there was no room in a classification yard to park them. Once a train was parked in a siding, its engines often were decoupled and driven to the classification yards to help remove some of the cars that had been sorted. The problem was that the newly assembled and powered trains had trouble leaving the classification yard, since there was no clear track for them to run on. The string of engineless cars left back in the siding created one more stretch of track that was occupied and unavailable for operations. Dispatchers quickly used up all the slack that existed in the rail system.

8. Frailey, "Union Pacific's Texas Traffic Jam," p. 26.

9. Englewood was a central north-south, east-west transfer point for freight moving to and from Mexico and for shipments to and from major Gulf coast petrochemical plants. The purpose of a classification yard is to gather freight cars from diverse locations, reassemble all cars going to a common location, provide power for the newly assembled train, and then send it on its way. Viewed from overhead, a classification yard has a treelike structure with a narrow trunk that fans out into numerous parallel tracks. Each track is associated with a different destination city. When a car is shoved up the tree trunk it is switched onto whichever track contains cars going to the same destination. As the tracks fill up, operators who do the switching have less freedom of movement and need to improvise by doing some switching outside the yard at a shipper's location, at a satellite yard, along the route to the destination, or by unusual sequences of moves. Any of these improvisations requires intimate knowledge of the yard and the surrounding area.

10. Frailey, "Union Pacific's Texas Traffic Jam," p. 29.

11. Frailey, "Union Pacific's Texas Traffic Jam," p. 29.

12. Frailey, "Union Pacific's Texas Traffic Jam," p. 30.

13. It has been well established that managers tend to attribute failure to external factors that are beyond their control but attribute success to their own efforts. What is striking in HROs is their tendency to reverse this pattern. They try to find internal reasons failure may have oc-

curred in order to identify levers they control and can change to reduce the likelihood of failure in the future. And although HROs take pride in their success, their feelings of pleasure are short-lived because they know that along with success come complacency, a temptation to reduce margins of safety, and inattentiveness. Success in an HRO typically is interpreted to mean that the errors being incubated out of sight have not yet lined up, reinforced one another, and interacted to produce a major disruption. Continued vigilance is the only safeguard against just such an interactively complex disruption.

14. Daniel Machalaba, "Union Pacific Struggles to Clear Up Delayed Shipments," *Wall Street Journal* (November 30, 1995): B4.

15. HROs, by contrast, allow decisions to migrate to those with expertise. People in HROs defer to those who know more than they do (see our discussion of the fifth HRO process of mindfulness, *deference to expertise*).

16. Machalaba, "Union Pacific Struggles to Clear Up Delayed Shipments," p. B4. This assurance can be interpreted as a clear example of people simplifying a complex issue, a practice that is just the *opposite* of what the better HROs do (see our discussion of the second HRO process, *reluctance to simplify interpretations*).

17. In the classic manner of throwing good money after bad, UP argues that their problems with bigness will solve themselves if they are allowed to get even bigger. It's a familiar story. *The business will take off if we get one more infusion of capital. The loan will get paid off if we get one more loan.* Perceiving that their reputation is on the line, UP argues that their wisdom in acquiring the CNW will be evident once they go further into debt and purchase the SP. What people, including those at UP, lose sight of is that the UP doesn't know how to implement a merger.

18. We are indebted to Paul Schulman for this point.

19. Allen R. Myerson, "Weary Hands at the Throttle," *New York Times* (April 26, 1998): 3.1.

20. Peter M. Senge, Art Kleiner, Charlotte Roberts, Richard B. Ross, and Bryan J. Smith, *The Fifth Discipline Fieldbook* (New York: Doubleday, 1994), pp. 235–293.

21. Zellner, "An Old Brakeman Faces His Ultimate Test," pp. 110–115.

22. Jack Burke, "Burns Out at UP," *Traffic World* (November 11, 1996): 30.

23. Ira Rosenfeld, "Mike Walsh Bows Out at UP, VP Davidson to Head Railroad," *Traffic World* (August 12, 1991): 10–11.

24. Daniel E. Maurino, James Reason, Neil Johnston, and Rob B. Lee, *Beyond Aviation Human Factors* (Aldershot, Hants, England: Ashgate, 1998), p. 14.

25. The contrast between dealing with the unexpected by means of anticipation and dealing with the unexpected by means of resilience comes from Aaron Wildavsky, *Searching for Safety* (New Brunswick, N.J.: Transaction, 1991). Given the existence of unexpected risks, one has to choose between *anticipation,* which is understood as "sinking resources into specific defenses against particular anticipated risks" and *resilience,* which is understood as "retaining resources in a form sufficiently flexible—storable, convertible, malleable—to cope with whatever unanticipated harms might emerge" (see p. 220). As Wildavsky explains, "Where risks are highly predictable and verifiable, and remedies are relatively safe, anticipation makes sense; most vaccines fit this criterion of efficient anticipation. Where risks are highly uncertain and speculative, and remedies do harm, however, resilience makes more sense because we cannot know which possible risks will actually become manifest" (see p. 221). Our own personal bias, and the tendency that we think we see in HROs, is to invest in knowledge and command over resources in the belief that this will enable us to mobilize a flexible response to the unexpected. Hence, we try to anticipate the unexpected but we do so by developing our capability for resilience. This means that we maintain an ongoing commitment to improve self-knowledge, relational knowledge, content knowledge, and capabilites to act thinkingly.

26. Myerson, "Weary Hands at the Throttle," p. 3.1.

27. Karlene H. Roberts, Susanne K. Stout, and Jennifer J. Halpern, "Decision Dynamics in Two High Reliability Military Organizations," *Management Science 40* (1994): 614–624; see p. 622.

28. Turner and Pidgeon, *Man-Made Disasters,* pp. 136–140.

29. Kathleen M. Eisenhardt, "High Reliability Organizations Meet High Velocity Environments: Common Dilemmas in Nuclear Power Plants," in *New Challenges to Understanding Organizations,* edited by Karlene H. Roberts (New York: Macmillan, 1993), pp. 117–136, quote from p. 121.

30. Eisenhardt, "High Reliability Organizations Meet High Velocity Environments: Common Dilemmas in Nuclear Power Plants," p. 124.

Chapter Two

1. Karl E. Weick and Karlene H. Roberts, "Collective Mind in Organizations: Heedful Interrelating on Flight Decks," *Administrative Science Quarterly 38* (1993): 357–381. Quote on p. 357.
2. K.E.W. is indebted to Gene Rochlin, Karlene Roberts, and Tom Mercer for their help in understanding how carriers work.
3. *To Err Is Human: Building a Safer Health System,* edited by L. T. Kohn, J. M. Corrigan, and M. S. Donaldson (Washington, D.C.: National Academy Press, 1999); see pp. 160–162.
4. The quotation is found on p. 37 in James Reason, *Managing the Risks of Organizational Accidents* (Aldershot, Hants, England; Brookfield, Vt., U.S.A.: Ashgate, 1997). The background for this depiction is found in Karl E. Weick, "Organizational Culture as a Source of High Reliability," *California Management Review 2* (1987): 112–127.
5. This cluster of activities has been discussed in the social science literature under labels such as team mind (see, for example, Richard Klimoski and Susan Mohammed, "Team Mental Model: Construct or Metaphor," *Journal of Management 20* [1994]: 403–437), heedful interrelating (Weick and Roberts, "Collective Mind in Organizations: Heedful Interrelating on Flight Decks"), respectful interaction (Karl E. Weick, "The Collapse of Sensemaking in Organizations: The Mann Gulch Disaster," *Administrative Science Quarterly 38* [1993]: 628–52), group mind (Lloyd E. Sandelands and Ralph E. Stablein, "The Concept of Organization Mind," in *Research in the Sociology of Organizations,* Vol. 5, edited by S. Bacharach and N. DiTomaso [Greenwich, Conn: JAI, 1987], pp. 135–161), and transactive memory (Daniel M. Wegner, "Transactive Memory: A Contemporary Analysis of Group Mind," in *Theories of Group Behavior,* edited by B. Mullen and G. R. Goethals [New York: Springer, 1987], pp. 185–208).
6. Gene I. Rochlin, "Informal Organizational Networking as a Crisis-Avoidance Strategy: U.S. Naval Flight Operations as a Case Study," *Industrial Crisis Quarterly 3* (1989): 159–176. Quote on p. 167.

□

7. Paul R. Schulman, "The Analysis of High Reliability Organizations: A Comparative Framework," in *New Challenges to Understanding Organizations,* edited by Karlene H. Roberts (New York: Macmillan, 1993), pp. 33–53. Quote on p. 36.

8. Our discussion of properties of expectations draws on James M. Olson, Neal J. Roese, and Mark P. Zanna, "Expectancies," in *Social Psychology Handbook of Basic Principles,* edited by E. T. Higgins and A. W. Kruglanski (New York: Guilford, 1996).

9. In this chapter we treat expectations and expectancies as synonyms, and use the word *expectation* unless material that is quoted uses the word *expectancy,* as is true in this case.

10. Olson, Roese, and Zanna, "Expectancies," p. 220.

11. This and other carrier practices are described in George C. Wilson, *Super Carrier: An Inside Account of Life Aboard the World's Most Powerful Ship, the USS John F. Kennedy* (New York: Macmillan, 1986). The discussion of a FOD walkdown is found on pp. 16–17.

12. Lee Clarke, "The Disqualification Heuristic: When Do Organizations Misperceive Risk?" *Research in Social Problems and Public Policy* 5 (1993): 289–312. The basic idea is that people disqualify disconfirming information, highlight confirming information, neglect information that contradicts a conviction, all in the interest of reducing uncertainty and increasing a sense of control.

13. This is sometimes referred to as *the positive-test strategy* and is discussed on pp. 112–120 in Ziva Kunda, *Social Cognition: Making Sense of People* (Cambridge, Mass.: MIT Press, 1999).

14. This sequence is adapted from p. 117 of Barry A. Turner and Nick F. Pidgeon, *Man-Made Disasters,* 2nd ed. (Oxford, UK: Butterworth-Heinemann, 1997).

15. Brian J. Kylen, "What Business Leaders Do—Before They Are Surprised," in *Advances in Strategic Management,* Vol. 3, edited by R. Lamb and P. Shrivastava (Greenwhich, Conn.: JAI), pp. 181–222.

16. Diane Vaughan, *The* Challenger *Launch Decision: Risky Technology, Culture and Deviance at NASA* (Chicago, Ill.: University of Chicago Press, 1996). See pp. 124, 141, 143, 179.

17. Vaughan, *The* Challenger *Launch Decision,* p. 249.

18. Adapted from Ellen J. Langer, "Minding Matters: The Consequences of Mindlessness-Mindfulness," in *Advances in Experimental Social*

Psychology 22, edited by L. Berkowitz (San Diego: Academic Press, 1989), pp. 137–173.

19. Karl E. Weick, "The Attitude of Wisdom: Ambivalence as the Optimal Compromise," in *Organizational Wisdom and Executive Courage,* edited by S. Srivastva and D. L. Cooperrider (San Franciso: Lexington, 1998), pp. 40–64.

20. Rochlin, "Informal Organizational Networking as a Crisis-Avoidance Strategy: U.S. Naval Flight Operations as a Case Study."

Chapter Three

1. Paul R. Schulman, "The Negotiated Order of Organizational Reliability," *Administration and Society 25* (1993): 353–372. Quote on p. 355.

2. Schulman, "The Negotiated Order of Organizational Reliability," pp. 357–358.

3. Schulman, "The Negotiated Order of Organizational Reliability," p. 356.

4. Henry Mintzberg, *The Rise and Fall of Strategic Planning* (New York: Free Press, 1994). See especially Chapter 5.

5. John S. Carroll, "Organizational Learning Activities in High-Hazard Industries: The Logics Underlying Self-Analysis," *Journal of Management Studies 35* (1998): 699–717.

6. *New York Times* (June 25, 2000), Section 3, p. 1.

7. William H. Starbuck and Frances J. Milliken, "*Challenger:* Fine-Tuning the Odds Until Something Breaks," *Journal of Management Studies 25* (1988): 319–340. A number of other scholars have documented the liabilities of success. See, for example, Danny Miller, "The Architecture of Simplicity," *Academy of Management Review 18* (1993): 116–138; and Sim B. Sitkin, "Learning Through Failure: The Strategy of Small Losses," in *Research in Organizational Behavior,* Vol. 14, edited by B. M. Staw and L. L. Cummings (Greenwich, Conn.: JAI), pp. 231–266.

8. John Carroll, "Organizational Learning Activities in High-Hazard Industries: The Logics Underlying Self-Analysis," p. 704.

9. Paul R. Schulman, "The Analysis of High Reliability Organizations: A Comparative Framework," in *New Challenges to Understanding*

Organizations, edited by Karlene H. Roberts (New York: Macmillan, 1993), pp. 33–53.

10. E. A. Cohen and J. Gooch, *Military Misfortunes: The Anatomy of Failure in War* (New York: Vintage, 1990), p. 44.

11. Ron Westrum, "Cultures with Requisite Imagination," in *Verification and Validation of Complex Systems: Human Factors Issues,* edited by J. A. Wise, D. Hopkin, and P. Stager (Berlin: Springer-Verlag, 1992), pp. 401–416. Material drawn from pp. 402–405.

12. Martin Landau and Donald Chisholm, "The Arrogance of Optimism: Notes on Failure Avoidance Management," *Journal of Contingencies and Crisis Management 3* (1995): 67–80.

13. Amy C. Edmondson, "Psychological Safety and Learning Behavior in Work Teams," *Administrative Science Quarterly 44* (1999): 350–383.

14. Schulman, "The Analysis of High Reliability Organizations: A Comparative Framework," p. 43.

15. Schulman, "The Analysis of High Reliability Organizations: A Comparative Framework," p. 47.

16. Schulman, "The Analysis of High Reliability Organizations: A Comparative Framework," p. 44.

17. Karl E. Weick, "Organizational Culture as a Source of High Reliability," *California Management Review 2* (1987): 112–127; quote on p. 116.

18. Schulman,"The Analysis of High Reliability Organizations: A Comparative Framework," pp. 46–47.

19. Rhona Flin, *Sitting in the Hot Seat: Leaders and Teams for Critical Incident Management* (Chichester: Wiley, 1996), pp. 10–15.

20. Regina F. Maruca, "Fighting the Urge to Fight Fires," *Harvard Business Review 77* (December 1999): 30–31.

21. See Scott D. Sagan, *The Limits of Safety: Organizations, Accidents, and Nuclear Weapons* (Princeton, N.J.: Princeton University Press, 1993), for a discussion of redundancies.

22. Larry Hirschhorn, "Hierarchy Versus Bureaucracy: The Case of a Nuclear Reactor," in *New Challenges to Understanding Organizations,* edited by Karlene H. Roberts (New York: Macmillan, 1993), pp. 137–150.

23. Kathleen M. Eisenhardt, "High Reliability Organizations Meet High Velocity Environments: Common Dilemmas in Nuclear Power Plants,"

in *New Challenges to Understanding Organizations,* edited by Karlene H. Roberts (New York: Macmillan, 1993), pp. 117–136.

24. Karlene H. Roberts, "Structuring to Facilitate Migrating Decisions in Reliability Enhancing Organizations," in *Advances in Global High-Technology Management,* Vol. 2, edited by L. R. Gomez-Mejia and M. W. Lawless (Greenwich, Conn.: JAI), pp. 171–191; quote on p. 183.

25. Schulman, "The Negotiated Order of Organizational Reliability," p. 364.

26. Mathilde Bourrier, "Organizing Maintenance at Two Nuclear Power Plants," *Journal of Contingencies and Crisis Management 21* (1996): pp. 104–112.

27. Eisenhardt, "High Reliability Organizations Meet High Velocity Environments: Common Dilemmas in Nuclear Power Plants," p. 132.

28. Eisenhardt, "High Reliability Organizations Meet High Velocity Environments: Common Dilemmas in Nuclear Power Plants," pp. 124-125.

29. Eisenhardt, "High Reliability Organizations Meet High Velocity Environments: Common Dilemmas in Nuclear Power Plants," pp. 124-125.

30. James T. Reason, *Managing the Risks of Organizational Accidents* (Aldershot, Hants, England; Brookfield, Vt., U.S.A.: Ashgate, 1997), p. 25.

31. William H. Starbuck, "Strategizing in the Real World," *International Journal of Technology Management 8* (1993): 77–85.

32. Schulman, "The Negotiated Order of Organizational Reliability," p. 362.

33. This perspective is found in Chapter 6 of Aaron Wildavsky, *Searching for Safety* (New Brunswick, N.J.: Transaction, 1991). Chapter 6 is titled, "Does Adding Safety Devices Increase Safety in Nuclear Power Plants?"

34. Lee Clarke, *Mission Improbable: Using Fantasy Documents to Tame Disaster* (Chicago: The University of Chicago Press, 1999).

35. Reason, *Managing the Risks of Organizational Accidents,* p. 49.

36. Hirschhorn, "Hierarchy Versus Bureaucracy: The Case of a Nuclear Reactor," p. 139.

37. Hirschhorn, "Hierarchy Versus Bureaucracy: The Case of a Nuclear Reactor," p. 139.

38. Wildavsky, *Searching for Safety,* p. 120.

39. The resilience practices in this paragraph are taken from Paul R. Schulman, "The Negotiated Order of Organizational Reliability," pp. 364–365.

40. Schulman, "The Negotiated Order of Organizational Reliability," p. 362.
41. Gene I. Rochlin, "Informal Organizational Networking as a Crisis-Avoidance Strategy: U.S. Naval Flight Operations as a Case Study," *Industrial Crisis Quarterly 3* (1989): 159–176.
42. This example draws from Robert F. Hartley, *Management Mistakes and Successes* (New York: Wiley, 2000), pp. 59–74.
43. Roberts, "Structuring to Facilitate Migrating Decisions in Reliability Enhancing Organizations," pp. 171–191.
44. See Karlene H. Roberts, Susanne K. Stout, and Jennifer J. Halpern, "Decision Dynamics in Two High Reliability Military Organizations," *Management Science 40* (1994): 614–624; and Karlene H. Roberts, "Structuring to Facilitate Migrating Decisions in Reliability Enhancing Organizations," pp. 171–191.
45. Roberts, "Structuring to Facilitate Migrating Decisions in Reliability Enhancing Organizations," p. 179.
46. Bourrier, "Organizing Maintenance at Two Nuclear Power Plants," pp. 104–112.
47. Ron Westrum, "Social Factors in Safety-Critical Systems," in *Human Factors in Safety Critical Systems,* edited by R. Redmill and J. Rajan (London: Butterworth-Heinemann, 1997), pp. 233–256.
48. Kathleen M. Eisenhardt, "Making Fast Strategic Decisions in High-Velocity Environments," *Academy of Management Journal 32* (1989): 543–576; quote on p. 570.
49. Reference to a study conducted by Anthem Blue Cross Blue Shield of Ohio reported in the *Wall Street Journal* (April 1999): A.1.
50. Mintzberg, *The Rise and Fall of Strategic Planning,* pp. 5–12.
51. Mintzberg, *The Rise and Fall of Strategic Planning,* pp. 227–254.
52. Schulman, "The Negotiated Order of Organizational Reliability," pp. 353–372.
53. Richard J. Hackman and Ruth Wageman, "Total Quality Management: Empirical, Conceptual, and Practical Issues," *Administrative Science Quarterly 40* (1995): 309–343.
54. W. Edwards Deming, *Quality, Productivity, and Competitive Position* (Cambridge, Mass.: MIT, Center for the Advanced Engineering Study, 1982).

55. Sim B. Sitkin, Kathleen M. Sutcliffe, and Roger Schroeder, "Distinguishing Control from Learning in Total Quality Management: A Contingency Perspective," *Academy of Management Review 18* (1994): 537–564.

Chapter Four

1. Robert E. Allinson, *Global Disasters: Inquiries into Management Ethics* (New York: Prentice Hall, 1993), p. 11.
2. Allinson, *Global Disasters: Inquiries into Management Ethics,* p. 193.
3. Allinson, *Global Disasters: Inquiries into Management Ethics,* p. 193.
4. *Webster's Dictionary of Synonyms*, 1st ed. (Springfield, Mass.: Merriam, 1951), p. 676.
5. Ellen J. Langer, "Minding Matters: The Consequences of Mindlessness-Mindfulness," in *Advances in Experimental Social Psychology,* V. 22, edited by L. Berkowitz (San Diego: Academic Press, 1989), pp. 137–173.
6. Ron Westrum, "Organizational and Inter-Organizational Thought," paper presented at the World Bank Conference on Safety Control and Risk Management, 1988.
7. Charles Perrow, *Normal Accidents: Living with High-Risk Technologies* (New York: Basic Books, 1984).
8. See Scott D. Sagan, *The Limits of Safety: Organizations, Accidents, and Nuclear Weapons* (Princeton, N.J.: Princeton University Press, 1993), p. 34.
9. Sagan, *The Limits of Safety: Organizations, Accidents, and Nuclear Weapons,* p. 33.
10. See James T. Reason, *Managing the Risks of Organizational Accidents* (Aldershot, Hants, England; Brookfield, Vt., U.S.A.: Ashgate, 1997), p. 91.

Chapter Five

1. Barry A. Turner and Nick F. Pidgeon, *Man-Made Disasters,* 2nd ed. (Oxford, England: Butterworth-Heinemann, 1997), p. 47.
2. Turner and Pidgeon, *Man-Made Disasters,* p. 102.

3. Edgar H. Schein, *Organizational Culture and Leadership* (San Francisco: Jossey-Bass, 1985). Definition is adapted from Chapter 1.

4. This close blending of culture with expectations has been noted by other researchers of culture such as Charles A. O'Reilly and Jennifer A. Chatman, "Culture as Social Control: Corporations, Cults, and Commitment," in *Research in Organizational Behavior,* Vol. 18, edited by B. M. Staw and L. L. Cummings (Greenwich, Conn.: JAI, 1996), on p. 160, who describe culture as a social control system based on shared norms and values that set expectations about appropriate attitudes and behavior for members of the group. Also see Mary Jo Hatch, "The Dynamics of Organizational Culture," *Academy of Management Review 18* (1993): 657–693. Hatch, who has made important extensions of Schein's ideas, has paid close attention to how assumptions are manifest in values and how values are realized in artifacts. She notes that "assumptions provide expectations that influence perceptions, thoughts, and feelings about the world and the organization. These perceptions, thoughts, and feelings are then experienced as reflecting the world and the organization. Members recognize among these reflections aspects they both like and dislike, and on this basis they become conscious of their values (without necessarily being conscious of the basic assumptions on which their experiences and values are based). . . . [R]ealization follows manifestation only if expectations and their associated values find their way into activity that has tangible outcomes. Many different activities can contribute to the realization of expectations: among them are the production of objects (e.g. company products, official reports, internal newsletters, buildings); engagement in organizational events (e.g. meetings, company picnics, award banquets, office parties); participation in discourse (e.g. formal speeches, informal conversation, joking)" (pp. 662, 666).

5. Interview in *Fast Company* (February-March 1998).

6. Thomas J. Peters and Robert H. Waterman Jr., *In Search of Excellence: Lessons from America's Best-Run Companies* (New York: HarperCollins, 1982), p. 322.

7. Charles O'Reilly, "Corporations, Culture, and Commitment: Motivation and Social Control in Organizations," *California Management Review 31* (1989): 9–25; quote on p. 16.

8. Edgar H. Schein, *The Corporate Culture Survival Guide* (San Francisco: Jossey-Bass, 1999); quote on p. 189.

9. *To Err Is Human: Building a Safer Health System,* edited by L. T. Kohn, J. M. Corrigan, and M. S. Donaldson (Washington, D.C.: National Academy Press, 1999).

10. *To Err Is Human: Building a Safer Health System,* p. 14.

11. James T. Reason, *Managing the Risks of Organizational Accidents* (Aldershot, Hants, England; Brookfield, Vt., U.S.A.: Ashgate, 1997), p. 194.

12. Reason, *Managing the Risks of Organizational Accidents,* pp. 191–222.

13. James T. Reason, "Achieving a Safe Culture: Theory and Practice," *Work and Stress 12* (1998): 293–306. See p. 294.

14. Andrew Hopkins, *Managing Major Hazards: The Lessons of the Moura Mine Disaster* (Sydney: Allen and Unwin, 1999).

15. Reason, *Managing the Risks of Organizational Accidents,* p. 195.

16. Reason, "Achieving a Safe Culture: Theory and Practice," p. 303.

17. Reason, *Managing the Risks of Organizational Accidents,* p. 11.

18. Hopkins, *Managing Major Hazards: The Lessons of the Moura Mine Disaster.*

19. Hopkins, *Managing Major Hazards: The Lessons of the Moura Mine Disaster,* p. 56.

20. Hopkins, *Managing Major Hazards: The Lessons of the Moura Mine Disaster,* p. 64.

21. Hopkins, *Managing Major Hazards: The Lessons of the Moura Mine Disaster,* p. 66.

22. Turner and Pidgeon, *Man-Made Disasters,* p. 188.

23. Reason, *Managing the Risks of Organizational Accidents,* pp. 213–218.

24. Andrew Hopkins, "Counteracting the Cultural Cause of Disaster," *Journal of Contingencies and Crisis Management 7* (1999): 141–149; quote on pp. 146–147.

25. George Mandler, *Mind and Body* (New York: Norton, 1984). Learned helplessness is discussed on pp. 244–248.

26. The following example comes from Gary Klein, *Sources of Power: How People Make Decisions* (Cambridge, Mass.: MIT Press, 1998), p. 274.

27. Robert L. Helmreich and Ashleigh C. Merritt, *Culture Work in Aviation and Medicine* (Aldershot, Hants, England: Ashgate, 1998); quote on p. 129.

28. Why $65? It cost Continental $5 million a month for being late (for example, payments for housing and meals for those who missed connections, payments to other airlines, crew overtime). If you're on time you save $5 million. Take half of that sum and give it back to the employees ($2.5 million divided by 40,000 people = $65 per month). See pp. 102–103 in Gordon Bethune, *From Worst to First* (New York: John Wiley, 1998).

29. Bethune, *From Worst to First,* p. 138.

30. Schein, *The Corporate Culture Survival Guide,* pp. 124–126.

31. James T. Reason, "Safety Paradoxes and Safety Culture," *Injury Control and Safety Promotion 7* (2000): 3–14; quote on p. 11.

Chapter Six

1. These estimates come from Lawrence H. Kaufman, "UP's Catch-Up Strategy, " in *Railway Age* (November 1, 1999) and Laura Goldberg, "After a Disastrous Bout of Gridlock and Controversial Merger, Railroad Has Most of Its Cars in Line Now Rolling Forward: Union Pacific Back on Track," *Houston Chronicle* (November 21, 1999).

2. We are grateful to Joann Sokkar and Catherine Augustine for their help in compiling and summarizing material on the Union Pacific Railroad.

3. Material taken from pp. 1–2 of 1998 Annual Report for Union Pacific.

4. Steve Jordon, "Chief Executive Leads Union Pacific Railroad Through Good Times," *Omaha World-Herald* (November 1, 1999).

5. Jordon, "Chief Executive Leads Union Pacific Railroad Through Good Times."

6. Goldberg, "After a Disastrous Bout of Gridlock and Controversial Merger, Railroad Has Most of Its Cars in Line Now Rolling Forward: Union Pacific Back on Track."

7. This discussion is based on Lawrence H. Kaufman, "UP's Catch-Up Strategy. "

8. See Karl E. Weick and Karlene H. Roberts, "Collective Mind in Organizations: Heedful Interrelating on Flight Decks," *Administrative Science Quarterly 38* (1993): 357–38, where a more technical version of this same idea is rendered in the form of a discussion of collective mind.

9. Quotation is from p. 2 of 1998 Annual Report for Union Pacific.

10. Jeffrey Pfeffer and Gerald R. Salancik, "Organizational Design: The Case for a Coalition Model of Organizations," *Organizational Dynamics* (Autumn 1977), pp. 18–19.

11. The "nominal group technique" is a process that enables a group to generate a list of issues, problems, or solutions and to come to some agreement on the relative importance of these issues. The process allows for equal participation by all members of a group and puts quiet team members on equal footing with more dominant members. The process consists of a number of steps but goes something like this. First, generate a list of issues, problems, and solutions—have people write out their statements (or to verbalize them if people feel safe to bring up controversial issues). Write the statements on a flipchart or board, eliminate duplicates and clarify the meaning of the statements. Next record the final list of statements on a flipchart or board and assign them a number or letter. The next step is for each group member to record the corresponding letters for each statement and rank order them. Finally, combine the rankings of all the group members. The higher the resulting number for a statement, the higher its ranking (priority).

12. Quotation comes from p. 114 of Suzy Wetlaufer, "Organizing for Empowerment: An Interview with AES's Roger Sant and Dennis Bakke," *Harvard Business Review* (Jan.-Feb. 1999), pp. 110–123.

13. For a discussion of media richness see Richard L. Daft and Robert H. Lengel, "Information Richness: A New Approach to Manager Information Processing and Organization Design," in *Research in Organizational Behavior,* Vol. 6, edited by B. M. Straw and L. L. Cummings (Greenwich, Conn.: JAI, 1984), pp. 191–233.

14. Aaron Wildavsky, *Searching for Safety* (New Brunswick, N.J.: Transaction, 1991), p. 120.

15. Pat Lagadec, *Preventing Chaos in a Crisis: Strategies for Prevention, Control, and Damage Limitation* (London: McGraw-Hill International, 1993), p. 54.

The Authors

Karl E. Weick is the Rensis Likert Collegiate Professor of Organizational Behavior and Psychology and professor of psychology at the University of Michigan. He joined the Michigan faculty in 1988 after previous faculty positions at the University of Texas, Cornell University, University of Minnesota, and Purdue University. His Ph.D. is from Ohio State University in social and organizational psychology. He is a former editor of the journal *Administrative Science Quarterly* (1977–1985), former associate editor of the journal *Organizational Behavior and Human Performance* (1971–1977), and current topic editor for human factors at the journal *Wildfire*.

Dr. Weick's book *The Social Psychology of Organizing*, first published in 1969 and revised in 1979, was designated one of the nine best business books ever written by *Inc.* Magazine in December 1996. This work has also been profiled in *Wired Magazine* and by Peters and Waterman in their book, *In Search of Excellence*. The organizing formulation has more recently been expanded into a book titled *Sensemaking in Organizations* (Sage, 1995). Weick was presented with the Irwin Award for Distinguished Scholarly Contributions by the Academy of Management in

1990. In the same year he received the Best Article of the Year award from the Academy of Management Review for his article "Theory Construction as Disciplined Imagination."

Dr. Weick's research interests include collective sense-making under pressure, medical errors, handoffs and transitions in dynamic events, high reliability performance, improvisation, and continuous change. His current writing is distributed across a variety of projects that include a re-analysis of the Dude wildland fire in 1990 in which six fire fighters perished, a discussion of mechanisms for intellectual renewal used by organizational scholars, a review of lessons learned about leadership from wildland fire tragedies, and a generalization of findings from research on high reliability organizations to the larger issue of high-performing organizations. Dr. Weick's graduate-level teaching focuses on the craft of scholarship, the social psychology of organizing, and micro foundations of organization studies. His courses in executive education focus on the management of uncertainty through sensemaking and improvisation.

Kathleen M. Sutcliffe is an associate professor of organizational behavior and human resource management at the University of Michigan Business School. She received a bachelor's degree from the University of Michigan, a master's degree from the University of Washington, and in 1991 a doctorate in management from the University of Texas at Austin. Before completing her doctorate, she lived and worked in Juneau, Alaska, as a program consultant for the State of Alaska and in Anchorage as a senior manager for one of the regional Alaska Native corporations.

In 1996 Dr. Sutcliffe received the NBD Bancorp Assistant Professor of Business Administration award for research excellence from the University of Michigan Business School. Her research interests include cognitive and experiential diversity in top management teams; team and organizational learning; how an organization's design affects its members' abilities to sense, cope with, and respond to changing demands; and organizational reliability and high performance. Her most recent work examines how elements of an organizational system influence errors in health care settings.

Dr. Sutcliffe teaches the core course on the fundamentals of human and organizational behavior to first-year MBA students at the University of Michigan Business School and also teaches courses in executive education. Her research has been published in the *Academy of Management Review, Academy of Management Journal, Human Communication Research, Leader to Leader, Organization Science, Strategic Management Journal,* and elsewhere.

Index